Through the Eyes of a Child

Sept. 9, 2012

To Emalise

Enjoy a good life!

Through the Eyes of a Child

"DIARY OF AN ELEVEN YEAR OLD JEWISH GIRL"

Ilse Reiner

Library of Congress Control Number:		2006909282
ISBN 10:	Hardcover	1-4257-3832-X
	Softcover	1-4257-3831-1
ISBN 13:	Hardcover	978-1-4257-3832-7
	Softcover	978-1-4257-3831-0

To order additional copies of this book, contact:
Xlibris Corporation
1-888-795-4274
www.Xlibris.com
Orders@Xlibris.com

37147

Contents

Introduction

While living in a Jewish orphanage in Prague, Czechoslovakia during the spring of 1942, and in anticipation of deportation to Terezin, I kept a diary since the age of eleven. In it I have recorded the lifestyle of all the children I lived with. Furthermore, I wrote about emotions such as love, hope and anger, but never of despair.

I finished my diary and was deported shortly thereafter. It was because of extreme luck, courage and deep faith in God that I have made it through there as well as through Birkenau/Auschwitz, and the labor camp Kurzbach in Silesia. I escaped from a death march leading to Gross Rosen with two women and hid in a farm cellar amidst piles of potatoes and burlap bags. Later on when the Russian military arrived, I masqueraded among the soldiers as a young male. After the war I walked a distance towards the Czech border where I finally collapsed. When I recovered, I found myself in a Red Cross van on the way to Prague, where I was hospitalized for three months. Thereafter I returned to my hometown of Vsetin where I lived with a Christian family, former friends of my mother's and mine as well. Their name was Lucas.

I immigrated to the USA in mid-October 1946 and made my residence in New York City.

I did not think about my diary until one day I read about the Precious Legacy exhibit from Prague coming to Washington, D.C. The exhibit opened in November of 1983 and I had been invited by the Smithsonian Institute to attend. I also received a party invitation from the Ambassador of the Czechoslovak Socialist Republic. By then I was totally dazed over the chain of events. In late June of 1990, I made a return trip to my homeland, accompanied by my daughter, Elaine. I managed to reestablish contact with one of the five Lukáš children who now, of course, were adults with youngsters of their own, even grandchildren. To my amazement, I learned of my diary's existence. When my daughter and I came to visit them the diary was returned to me. I must say that I stared at it in disbelief for quite some time. We slept that night in the very same house I once lived in and where the diary found a home through the Nazi and Communist occupation, years hidden in our wooden trunk, which was kept for safety with other belongings of ours in their attic.

When one of our friend's daughters became a teacher, she taught from my diary. Her name was Vera. She told me of the incredible impact it had on the children she taught when they learned that their teacher knew me—even lived with me. Though not too interested in the years of the Nazi regime, their interest rose considerably as they now could relate better to the plight of the Jewish children, their dignity and strength.

The Secretary of the Smithsonian Institution and Mrs. Ripley
The Chairman of the Board of Philip Morris Incorporated and Mrs. Weissman
The Director of the National Museum of Natural History and Mrs. Fiske
The Director of the Smithsonian Institution Traveling Exhibition Service

*request the pleasure of your company at a preview reception
in honor of the exhibition*

THE PRECIOUS LEGACY

JUDAIC TREASURES FROM THE CZECHOSLOVAK STATE COLLECTIONS

Tuesday, November eighth

*The National Museum of Natural History
Smithsonian Institution
Constitution Avenue at Tenth Street, N.W.
Washington, D.C.*

Reception, seven o'clock to nine o'clock

Rsvp by October twenty-eighth   *Black Tie*

The Precious Legacy Invitation

The international agreement between the Smithsonian Institution and the Czechoslovak Socialist Republic includes fifty-seven selections from the noted collection of art works created in Terezin (Theresienstadt) concentration camp. This part of *The Precious Legacy* will be shown at the B'nai B'rith Klutznick Museum.

You are cordially invited to view these works and to participate in a special memorial program at the B'nai B'rith Klutznick Museum preceding the dinner. The address is 1640 Rhode Island Avenue, NW, Washington, D.C.

Preview, Terezin Collections:	*5:30 p.m.*
Memorial Program:	*6:00 p.m.*

Preview Terezin Collection and Memorial Program

Honoring the exhibition "The Precious Legacy: Judaic Treasures from the Czechoslovak State Collections"

The Ambassador of the Czechoslovak Socialist Republic
and Mrs. Stanislav Suja
request the pleasure of the company of

Ms. Ilse Reiner

at a reception

on Wednesday, November 9, 1983

at 6,30   o'clock, p.m.

Embassy of the Czechoslovak
Socialist Republic
3900 Linnean Avenue

Regrets only
363-6315

Invitation from the Ambassador of the Czechoslovak Socialist Republic

4

Photo of Ilse's diary and flowers that were presented to her by the Lukas children upon her arrival back to her hometown, 44 years later.

DEDICATION

This diary is dedicated to the children who were sent to Terezin and to my late husband, Charlie, whose persuasive manner prompted me to translate the diary so that our children, Richie and Elaine would have a better grasp of my early childhood years.

Since then the diary has captivated young and old in the now Czech Republic and in the USA. It is my wish to make the subject of the diary known to children everywhere.

Acknowledgement

With special thanks to the late Frantisek and Lydia Lukáš from my hometown Vsetin in Moravia, for searching for me after the end of WWII and tracing me through the help of the repatriation bureau to a Prague hospital and offering me their home.

Also a heartfelt thank you to their five children, (the late son, Jan) and his sisters Vera, Marie, Eva, and Lydia who accepted me into their midst so warmly and treated me as their very own. We are close to this day. This relationship now also includes a daughter Olga, born to the couple after I had immigrated to the USA.

Family portrait of the Lukas Family

The Year 1939, The Nazis Infiltrate

One morning in March of 1939, men and women were standing in the streets of their town, Vsetin, Czechoslovakia, wiping the tears off their faces as their bewildered children were looking on. The elders were staring at German soldiers marching in goose step down from the train station where they had arrived by carloads a few minute earlier.

Singing as they passed us by on their way to the town square, we learned that our country was occupied and renamed to the "Protectorate of Bohemia and Moravia," with the Slovak part of the population breaking away from us, forming their own government headed by a Nazi sympathizer of Slovak origin.

Soon the red flags with swastikas were draped from the windows and the shops of Jewish merchants were padlocked. This act was followed by signs appearing on buildings with store fronts which read "Pure Aryan Establishment" with German women dressed in "dirndls" proudly promenading in our streets. The atmosphere among the native people grew tense as it became necessary to speak in whispers and use codes due to frequent arrests of innocent people.

I lived at that time with my parents in a villa named "Hubertus," surrounded by blooming shrubs in the garden which also had a gazebo I liked to sit in. I was nine years old at that time and aware of my parents exerting efforts to make various contacts, in order for us to be able to immigrate to the USA. They were aided in this matter by my mother's brother, who lived in New York City with his American wife of many years.

Time went on and very little progress had been made. My father became highly nervous. My parents' relationship had deteriorated. Unbeknown to me, they had personal difficulties back in 1936 which they had patched up. This time it was for real! How well I still remember the day when my mother asked me which parent I wanted to stay with. All three of us at that time were forced to live in the attic of our villa; the rest of our house being assigned by the Germans to a prominent Czech physician who, with his family, had to relocate from Brno to Vsetin in order to take care of the many families which migrated to our suburbs in order to work in a newly built munitions factory.

It was but a couple of days later that two Gestapo men showed up at our villa. They said that they came to take my father into "protective custody." They also took my father's brother, Uncle Rudolph, as I learned later on. Both of them were taken to the city of Brno and kept in a medieval castle turned into a notorious prison complex named **Spielberg**.

After that incident, mother and I took our possessions having lost most of them and hidden others, and we moved to a nearby village of Ruzdka, where we occupied one room and shared the toilet down the hall with two other families. Our landlady lived in a decent apartment adjacent to her grocery store. I became my mother's confidante in many ways and was growing up quickly due to circumstances around me.

One day the Gestapo showed up again and conducted a house search making a mess out of our room. They were searching for our stashed sugar and coal for their own needs as there was a great shortage of these items. Everything in those days was rationed. Furthermore, they confiscated some books we had on the shelf. Either the authors were Jewish or they did not agree with the subject matter the books dealt with. Fortunately, they had overlooked a couple of cactus plants on the window sill, for in the earth we had hidden some jewelry, which I am glad to say I have today.

Six weeks later my dad was released as was his brother. I heard him say he was forced to sign papers not to reveal what had taken place in Spielberg. Since mother still insisted on divorcing my father; and in fact, filed papers with an attorney to do so, father went to live with his brother Rudolph and his Christian wife and four children for the next several months. He then moved on to Prague and in September of 1942 was deported to Poland, his last and only postcard to me came from **Lublin**. The entire transport was ill-fated.

As for my mother, she was picked up by the Gestapo for questioning shortly after my father was discharged. She was kept away from me for one week during which time I stayed with my father, at his brother's house and at a later date arrested once more.

I was allowed to visit my mother once during the three weeks she was locked up in her cell and through contacts made by Terka, smuggled letters back and forth and some food to her as well. Thereafter, she was transferred to Brno and six weeks later sent to **Ravensbrück** in Fürstenberg, a province of Mecklenberg, Germany, the first women's concentration camp for political prisoners and later for Jews only. There she contracted tuberculosis. It was sometime in 1941 (late summer or early fall I think) that she was temporarily discharged. I received a letter from her which said that she was in the Jewish hospital in Prague which was on Kelleyova Street where her cousin Jenny worked. I was not allowed to visit my mom. By then I had to wear the *Star of David* and obtain a traveling permit. It was this and her contagious disease which had the doctors keep us apart.

We continued our close communication through letters and once again through Terka's help, frequent packages were sent to her with food bought on the black market. I also embroidered little things and sent them to her as well as photos. She phoned me once. This call upset both of us terribly. I screamed, "Momma, Momma" and she could hardly speak, trying to control her sobs. We did not see each other ever again. I guess I was 10½ by then.

On February 27, 1942 my mother died and was buried in Straslice adjacent to Olshany in the Jewish cemetery in Prague. Three weeks later, I was ordered by the German court to pack my suitcase, received a travel permit and was sent to live in a Jewish Orphanage in Prague.

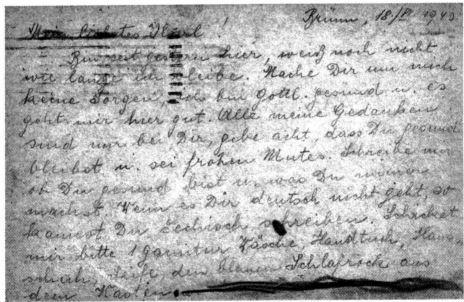

Postcard from my mother from the prison in Brno

BRÜNN   June 18, 1940
(Brno in czek, capital of Moravia)

My dearest Ilserl (german) in czek Ilsinko which is
the demunitive of ILSE

I have been here since yesterday and do not know
how long I will remain here. Do not worry about me.
I am fine here and doing well healthwise. All my
thoughts are with you. Take care of yourself so that
you stay healthy and remain optimistic. Write
to me and let me know if you are well and what
you are doing all the time. If you find german
too difficult, then write in czek. Please send me a
set of underware, a towel, slippers, soap and the blue
bathrobe from the closet. sentence crossed out by the censor
with a blue marker

   Second side (actually the front of the post card)
Is it possible to get some dry salami & the triangular cheese?
I will write now only once every fourteen days. However,
you may write more often. Visits are not permitted. My
gold and precious child. I am sending you many,
many kisses .   your Mommy
With warm regards to dear Terka.   (over)

Translation of postcard from Brunn

15

Postcard from my mother from the concentration camp Ravensbruck

Post card from Ravensbrück in Mecklenburg near the Danish border from the first women's concentration camp.

OCTOBER 1940

Dearest Ilsinko,

I am certain that by now you must have received my card which I have send you before any departure as well as my belongings. Do not worry about me. I am healthy and doing O.k. From now on you can write to me once per month only.

Kiss,
Mom

This card came as a big blow to me and my mother as well. Both of us felt that the political charges against her would be dismissed and that she would be comming home. Instead, she had to inform me that she was taken out of the country, far away from home and me!

Translation of postcard from Ravensbruck

**LETTERS WHICH ARE POORLY WRITTEN AND
NOT CLEAR ENOUGH FOR THE CENSORS TO READ SHALL BE DESTROYED**

Women's Concentration Camp RAVENSBRÜCK Fürstenberg by Mecklenburg	My exact address is: **Charlotte Eichner No. 4792 Block 13 Women's Concentration Camp Ravensbrück Fürstenberg by Mecklenburg** Mailing without the Number & Block will not be acceptable
Declaration of Ordinance **Camp Director** Notice from the management of the camp. Every prisoner is allowed once per month to receive a letter or a postcard. These must be written in ink and be clear and distinct. You may write on both sides but not to accede 15 lines. The sender must indicate her exact address, as well as number of the prisoner and cell block. You may enclose in every letter one postage stamp, any other shall be confiscated. Mail which does not comply with these requirements shall be destroyed. Letters must not be stuffed with anything. Packages which contain sending of money are permitted but must be by way of money orders. Money enclosure is strictly forbidden. Everything can be bought in the camp. NATIONAL SOCIALIST NEWSPAPERS are allowed, however, they must be requested personally by the prison inmate through the censors at the post office of the women's concentration camp. Sending of pictures and photos is forbidden. **From the camp Director**	

Translation of Rules and Regulations from the Women's Concentration Camp

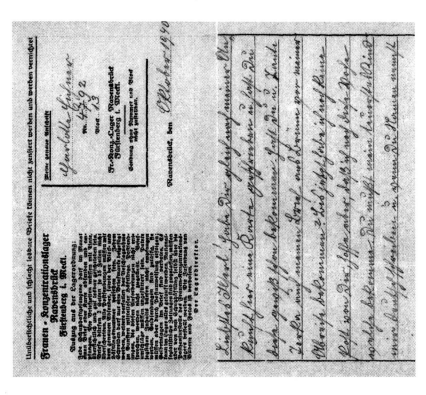

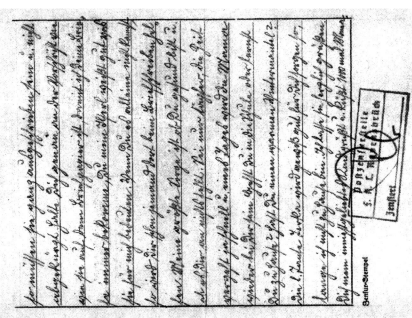

Letter of October 1940

Ravensbrück, OCTOBER 1940

Dearest Ilsinko,

I have send you a postcard immediately upon my arrival here. I am certain that by now you have received it. Have you and aunt Terka also received my letter from Brünn which I have written to you prior to my departure? Up to now, I have no mail from you but am hopefull that I will receive some this week yet. My most precious child, you must write to me very distinctly and when you write names, they must be written out entirely, no abreviations. Follow carefully the instructions as imprinted on front of this letter to assure my receiving your mail. You know Ilsinko well, what that means to me. If you can not write yourself, then someone at your end can assist you.

My great worry is that you should stay healthy and that you should not have to do without anything. Have courage for time passes quickly and one of these days your momma will be with you once again. Are you learning in school these days or are you studying at home? Do you have a warm winter coat? aunt Terka will surely look out well after you during my absence from home. I am sending her my heartfelt greetings.

As for you my one and only dearly beloved child, I am sending greetings along with a thousand kisses. Mamma.

stamp of the censor

Post office Censoring Division
F. K. L. Ravensbrück

Censored _____

date: 7-21-96 I'm Atlanta during the OLYMPICS translated from German into English by Ilsinka Eichner, now Ilse Reiner age 66, as she is approaching her 50th jubileum in the USA, come this OCTOBER '96

Translation of October 1940 letter.

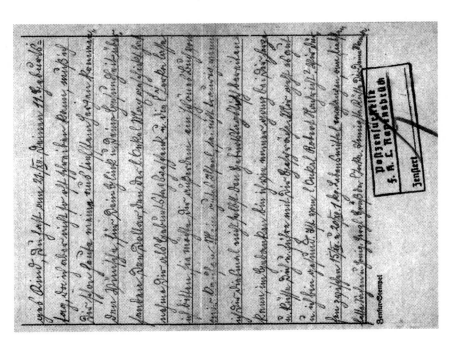

My mother's birthday wishes for my eleventh birthday.

Letter of NOVEMBER 1940

My precious Ilsinko,

I have received both your letters, which gave me a great deal of pleasure. I also thank aunt Terka for the few lines she added, putting my mind at ease. Furthermore I was pleased to learn that uncle Max has written to you. Ilsinka have you answered him? I was pleasantly surprised with the 20 Marks you have send me. I simply could not take my eyes of your writing. My sweet, dear one and only child, you will have your 11th birthday come Dec. 21st. Since I can not write too often I must now wish you from the bottom of my heart much happiness and mainly good health. I would appreciate if aunt Terka would buy you a birthday present from one with the dollar uncle Max send. My good little girl, do not be sad that I am not buying something for you myself, for in my thoughts I am always with you, kissing you and embracing you.

I am doing O.K. and am staying healthy. Is there any news from uncle Robert? We are allowed to receive a food parcel between Dec. 15th and Dec. 20st, weighing 1 kilo. What I would like best is   and honey. Warm regards to dear aunt Terka with many kisses from your Mom my

Translation of letter dated November 1940

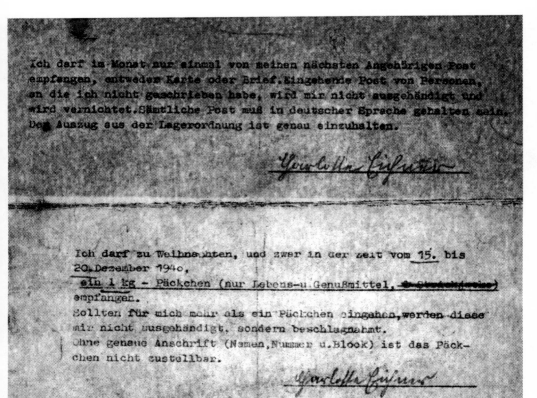

Regarding Christmas parcels.

The upper paragraph states:

> I can receive mail from the next of kin once per month only, be it a postcard or a letter. If mail is sent to me from someone I have not written to, it will not be delivered to me. It will be destroyed. All mail must be written in German only and the rules of the camp commander must be complied with.

(Signed by Charlotte Eichner—my mom)

The paragraph above indicates that the prisoners were allowed to receive Christmas packages from the December 15th through 20th of 1940 (food parcel of 1 kilo).

Explanation:

Uncle ~~that~~ was mother's <u>brother</u>. who lived in <u>the USA</u>. (NYC)
(Aunt) <u>aunt Adele</u> was my mother's <u>sister</u> and Max's <u>sister</u>.
She lived in Tchechich Teschen "Česky Těšín" the town <u>Leo</u>
came from and where also my grandmother's sister aunt
Angela lived. (she was simple, very gentle and blind by the
time I got to know her, I mean Angela, not Adele).

Aunt Terka was <u>not</u> a blood relative but since I was a
young child away from my own family, mom kept referring
to her in her letters to me as aunt Terka. Thus she must
have thought that I may feel closer to Terka and perhaps
less lonely. She was indeed very good to me and I liked
her fine.

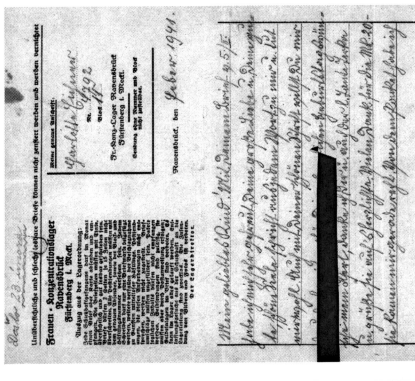

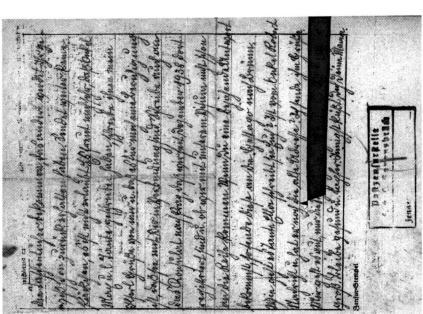

Letter of February 1941

Feb. 1941

My beloved child

I was very happy with your letter of Feb. 5th. Your beautiful soul and deep love for me penetrated through your writing and gave me immense joy. I was also pleased with your very nice handwriting. [CUT CUT CUT] Also many thanks
by sensor
for my birthday wishes. My warmest regards to aunt Terka. Thanks for the 20 Marks. It came in handy. From the parcel you have send one I received the handkerchiefs and the rest am sure was send back to you. Do not send me any packages as it is not allowed. I was very happy that uncle Max and auntie have written to you. Please Ilsinko write to them and give them my love. Tell them also that it is comforting for me to know that they are in touch with you.

Also write to the consulate in Prague and tell them that we were registered there since 1938 and see whether we got our visas yet. When you receive an answer from there forward it to the Gestapo in Brünn. How is aunt Adele! Do you hear from her? Is there any news from Robert and is he still at the old address! I send him my regards. I am doing fine, only [CUT CUT CUT]. — big. Stay healthy
by sensor
and chipper. Many hugs from your Mommy

(over)

Translation of February 1941 letter.

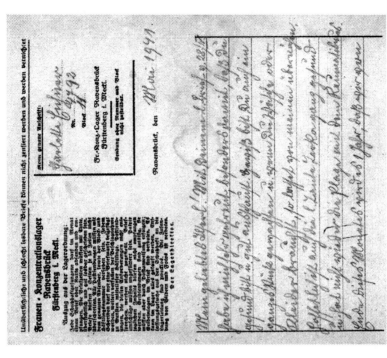

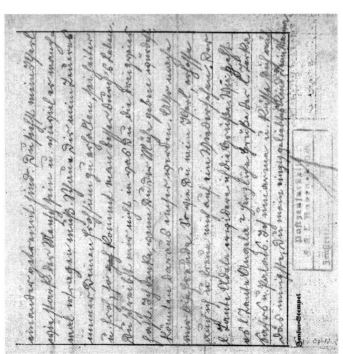

Letter of May 1941

27

May 1941

My beloved Ilsinko,

I was very happy with your letter of April 28. and especially pleased to learn that you are healthy and looking well. Surely you must have grown quite a bit and if you need to make over some of my dresses or underwear for yourself then do so.

Hopefully aunt Terke is feeling better and not bothered by rheumatism. At the end of this month it will be a year already, since we were separated from each other. You see my Ilsinko, how much strenght one needs and what one must endure at times. Be sure to hold on to your cheerfull disposition as it helps one to get through in life. You did not write to me what you got the two   in. (pertains to my school grades) I think if you try harder you can really do better. So please give me the pleasure.

Dear Ilsinko, I too look forward to us becomming reunited. How is aunt Adele? And how is aunt Angela? My best regards to Terka and the Sachars.

I am embracing you, hugging you and kissing you.

Your loving Mummy

(Adele was mom's sister, Angela was her aunt, my grandmother's sister)

Translation of May 1941 letter.

Profile Of Mother—Charlotte Eichner

My mother was born in Brenna, near Czech Teschen in Silesia. One of many siblings of Ignatz and Berta (called Betty) Eichner. She was serious by nature and kept a kosher household, thus pork products were never brought into the house and meat and dairy were not used together. She spoke Czech or German, was cultured and loved the opera. Her favorite was *Madame Butterfly* by **Puccini**. She also liked to sing German lieder which were often sad. On other occasions she sang children's songs in German or read to me fairy tales by **Brothers Grimm**.

I admired her beautiful embroidery and enjoyed thoroughly her home baked goodies, whether they were rich pastries, fancy torts or plain cookies. I loved her apple strudel the best!

She was a disciplinarian in our household and tended to my needs whether they were scholastic or recreational.

I was an only child and she did her best to instill good habits in me, one in particular was not to procrastinate, to do what I have to do today, for who knows what tomorrow will bring. I have never forgotten that! She emphasized cleanliness and neatness as well.

We went sledding together and ice skating. When the summer came, she taught me to swim. We played ping-pong and I was her little helper when she went to buy her fruits and vegetables mid-week in the downtown square; that was when the farmers brought their produce to town. I proudly carried my little basket while she had a large fishnet bag.

I loved my hikes with her, for it was fun going into the woods and look for mushrooms or pine cones, which were sometimes used as firewood. There were other times when we went picking berries—such simple fun! Later on we poured sweet cream over them and enjoyed the treat. On my birthday she sat with me at a table pouring hot cocoa into my china cups which I used for playing when catering to my favorite doll. I can still see her in my mind today, porcelain face, rosy cheeks, long lashes, wearing a beautiful pale organza dress with a matching hat, adorned with small multi-color rosebuds. I also had a cuddly baby doll.

Profile Of Father—Max Eichner

Father was born in Polish Teschen. He was quite opposite from my mother. One of five children, he cared very much about the good things in life. He was a sharp dresser and was always buying something for us whether we wanted it or not. He liked Persian rugs, bought nice paintings for the house, even china. Mom would sometimes complain about it. He loved comedy and to show me off. There were times when I would practice the piano with my mother sitting nearby. He would come in quietly with his violin under his arm and when I finished, he would play for us such happy, lively tunes.

Dad liked to go to soccer games and loved to take mom to concerts and operas. He was a compulsive card player and liked to play billiards as well. I think I was past the age of six when I started to notice that he always had a cigarette in his hand and drank one cup of black coffee after another. His teeth and fingertips had become stained which I did not like.

Then one day mom said that dad left for a few weeks to go to a sanatorium. I was told that he suffered from nicotine poisoning and coughed real bad. I did not understand what was happening. At the age of seven, I had a serious operation for a mastoid on the right ear preceded by scarlet fever. So life got a little bumpy but the next two years thereafter, as I recall, were pleasant until the age of nine and a half.

Prior to that, dad would always have a Sabbath dinner with us and would attend services mostly every Saturday morning in our small synagogue. Life was difficult and confusing for a young child who, due to circumstances, had to grow up faster than other children her age.

Portrayal Of Home Life And
Jewish Holidays

We had a maid called Loiska and she stayed with us a half a day throughout the week except for weekends. When father returned from the sanatorium things went on as usual. He helped to take care of me. Loiska cleaned and helped with the laundry. Mom would on occasion go away for a few days to a spa resort for healing different ills, hers was of a bronchial nature. Both parents made certain that I did not go to sleep at night without saying my prayers, which I recited in Hebrew.

I have pleasant memories of going with my father to the ballpark. While he cheered on the players, I enjoyed sipping soda and admiring the candy necklace he would always buy for me. He went to a synagogue frequently. Upon his return all three of us enjoyed a good meal, after which my mom would sit me down beside her as we jointly read out of a prayer book called Deborah. It was written in German and I needed help sometimes for it was not my native tongue. My parents were practicing Jews and taught me to be reverent as well. My mother kept a kosher home and Friday was very special to her. From early morning she busied herself with preparations for the Sabbath meal.

I could always count on the carp suddenly appearing and swimming in our bathtub. After she killed him I watched her preparing some clear gelatin and putting him in with large slices of carrots and halves of walnuts as well. No, I could not eat that dish! That evening I opted for her chicken soup with fine noodles and "Challa" she had baked earlier that day.

I watched my mother make the dough, braid it, then with a brush, paint egg white all over, so that the Challa would come out evenly brown and shiny. After that chore was finished, she went on to the next one, spraying starch on a previously washed table cloths before ironing it. It had to be white. Then she proceeded to polish the silver and the candlesticks in particular, until they would glisten. Slowly but surely a warm "heimishe" feeling would envelope the home and father would soon walk in with flowers. He washed his hands and put on a hat. We sat down to eat but not before mom lit the candles, circling her hands over them, then saying a blessing, while partially covering her eyes. I wondered why, yet never asked.

I was taught to say "brochas", the Hebrew blessings. I said one when it thundered, when it was lightening or when the rainbow would appear after a heavy rain soon followed by sunshine. Came *Rosh Hashanah*, the Jewish New Year, I said one as I was putting on a new dress prior to accompanying my parents to our temple for services. Of course, we went on foot not only because it was *Jom Tov*, and a Holy day rather than just a holiday, but also because only the two prominent physicians in town had cars. The rest of the townspeople rode bicycles or walked. When going to suburban communities there were two buses on the downtown square to be taken in either direction. Trains were used for long distances meaning two hours away or more. When we arrived for services, our mothers seated themselves separately from the fathers. Same room, but a higher platform on which the men sat, dividing them from the women with a wooden railing. The men's side was facing the pulpit or the sacred ark housing the *Torahs*, (scrolls of Jewish learning) while the women faced a small stained glass window instead. All seats I recall had name plates so that everyone knew where to sit.

After *Rosh Hashanah* came *Yom Kippur*, the most sacred day on the Jewish calendar. Everyone prayed and asked God for forgiveness for their sins and did not eat from the proceeding day at sundown until the sun set down again on the following day. The town florist was busy, for on this day women would receive small bouquets of flowers. My mother liked a simple bunch of violets surrounded by original leaves. They were her favorite. One year my father forgot to order them for her and got gladioli instead. Her embarrassment was immense as she kept looking at this conspicuous bouquet of flowers, reminding her of a big broomstick she said. I knew that she was angry with my father at that time. It was a bad beginning for the start of New Year. Not all women had flowers, some had apples with cloves stuck in them. It reminded me of a porcupine. All this was to prevent the fasting women from feeling faint by having a pleasant aroma in front of them to inhale periodically.

When "Jitzkor" occurred, the prayer for the dead, it was usually eleven o'clock or noon and we children had to leave the sanctuary. Since the rabbi and his wife known as the rebbetzin, also lived in the same small house whose forefront was our temple, we went into their garden filled with several apple trees. We talked and laughed enjoying the fresh air and at times the sunshine. Needless to say, to pull an apple and eat it was strictly forbidden to us, just like to Adam and Eve. It was a rule we abided by with great difficulty. We could not wait for services to end, hear the sound of the *shofar*, known also as the Ram's Horn and go home to take off our fineries and eat.

At "Succoth", or the holiday of thanks for harvest, we did nothing special but mom would cut off some branches of birch trees, bring them into the house and stick them behind pictures and mirrors on the wall. The following week came *Simchas Torah* at which time our parents prepared small packages of sweets and dried fruits. We received them after we marched around with flags of white and blue depicting the "Mogen David", known as the *Star of David*. We sang some kind of songs, don't recall what, and we were very happy! In December we always had to draw and color Christmas trees in school. While at home we looked forward to lighting the *Menorah*, one parent chanting the blessings, then all three of us would burst into song singing, *Maoz Tzur* which retold the miracle of the lights; mainly of the oil which burned for eight days. The warrior *Judea of Maccabee* and all the rest was still on my mind while taking off the wrapper from the chocolate coins. Presents on that night nor on the following nights were not given, but my father grated potatoes and fried the "latkes", known as potato pancakes in English. He sure made them good. With home made apple sauce they were a treat!

Purim is indeed a long "Megillah", a lengthy story but an interesting one. I learned of Mordechai, Queen Esther, her kind King, Ahasuerus and the treacherous Haman who was plotting the destruction of the Jews in which he did not succeed.

Mid-spring brought us the holiday of "Pesach", and we had matzos galore. This unleavened bread was crunchy. We observed the first two nights of the Seder with dinner rich in rituals and songs that can last forever. The youngest, mainly me, would read from the Haggadah and ask questions. This "Haggadah" written in Czech and Hebrew which I used then, is in my possession still today, though falling apart. Not having had grandparents or siblings, our Passover was rather quiet except for the occasional visitors who had no where else to go on that night. That about sums it up for the holidays as I remember them.

As for my studies in Judaic history and the Hebrew language, I learned it in the public school twice per week. Our rabbi's assistant, Mr. Reiss, would come and teach us, while the Christian children, mainly Catholics, were instructed in catechism by their own. This of course was conducted in separate classrooms.

I had three Jewish girlfriends whose home I went to often. I also had several Christian school friends whom I liked a great deal, one in particular. Her name was Vera, the daughter of Frantisek and Lydia Lukáš, who had four other daughters and a son, who was the oldest of the siblings. Years later another daughter was born to them. Her name was Olga. Mrs. Lukáš liked and respected my mother. She was a kind pious lady and hardworking. She hid some things for us when tough times came. After World War II, in May of 1945, I found myself in a hospital in Prague where I remained for three months; after which time the Lukášes became my benefactors and took me into their home where I remained until I immigrated to the USA.

The above is the **I.D. Card** I have been given upon my return to my hometown. I kept this document for all these years. For one, it has reinstated me to the status of a human being who had her rightful name again and was no longer just a number, something which I have refused to remember while in Birkenau/Auschwitz and Kurzbach as well. Secondly, it was simply a strange feeling of reality, too bewildering for me when looking at the I.D. and reading the following:

Date of Imprisonment:
From 24/10/1942 This means October 24, 1942
To 25/5/1955 May 5, 1945

My name: Ilse Eichnerova
Address: Vsetin No. 1111
Occupation: Student
Is a member of the **freed political prisoners** of Vsetin and its vicinity.

*The name of Holocaust survivor or victim was not coined as yet. So here I was a child of **fifteen**, a political prisoner. How bizarre I thought to myself.*

Rude Awakening

I kept thinking to myself what a perfect day it is as I sat down in the grass watching a few baby ducks waddling towards the nearby brook.

My mom is standing but a few feet further down from me bent over a laundry basket, pulling out clean sheets and towels which she is getting ready to hang on a clothesline which extends from there toward the back of the house where we live in one room, with one toilet, down the hall shared with two other families. It was not much but for now it was our home.

The sun is shining ever so brightly and the air is smelling from fresh cut grass. The scent of honeysuckle is whifting through the air which makes my nostrils quiver with much delight. I close my eyes for a while, my mind drifts dreamily into the distance, imagining how well I was going to sleep tonight on the sun bleached sheets and tucked in by my loving mom, when suddenly I was jarred back into reality by my mom's voice calling out to me.

I opened my eyes quickly and as my head turned slightly, I saw mom walking briskly towards me. Then I noticed two men dressed in tailored suits wearing tyroleam hats adorned by a small feather. They are walking at a slow pace towards us. When they stopped in front of us they flipped over their suit lapels thus exposing the small insignia of the swastika, which identified them as the very much feared Gestapo men. The chill ran up and down my spine as I looked from them to my mom noticing how pale she had suddenly become. Her hand was trembling as she reached out trying to draw me closer to her. The Gestapo are presently exchanging some words with my mom in German. Shortly thereafter she turns to me with these words, *"Ilsinko, moje drahè dite, neboj se a but statečná. Já Te musim na chvili opustit a nevim ješte kdy se k tobì budu moci vrácet!"* "Ilsinko, my beloved child, have no fear, show courage! For I have to go away from you for a while and don't know as yet when I will be able to return to you." When hearing these words from my mother's mouth I realized that my perfect day until now has been cut short. In my childlike bewilderment and with much anxiety in my voice I asked, "Momma, where are you going with these men?" She replied, "I am being taken to their headquarters in Vsetín for questioning, someone will come and be with you before the night falls." She walked with me to the house, packed some small necessities, took her raincoat, gave me a tight hug and walked out of the room, down the stairs. The Gestapo was waiting for her outside and soon thereafter I heard the sound of their automobile driving off with her, leaving a sharp pain in my heart. This was my mom's second arrest. I was left abandoned standing in a room crying bitterly.

I was only around ten years old and the only child of Charlotte and Max Eichner who made his living as a timber broker. Suddenly, I found myself without either parent, not knowing what to do.

I will not forget that day when my mother was taken away from me. How could I! How could any child! I was told that I was quite astute in my thinking, alert, intuitive, with a mind of a child beyond my young years of maturity, but this was just too much for me. The night had fallen when a kind woman by the name of Theresa (I called her Terka) came to be with me. I barely knew her. She looked after me with kindness throughout my mom's incarceration until her death. I became quite fond of her and my mom trusted her implicitly. She had known Terka before. I had been able to visit my mom only once after her arrest. Coaxed by Terka, I went to Vsetin to the Gestapo headquarters asking for permission to visit her. My coat pockets were slightly bulging with two sandwiches I hoped to be able to bring to her. With courage in my heart I entered the fairly large office headquarters and approached the Gestapo. When I told one of them why I came he raised the tone of his voice angrily, "Why don't you speak German?" I complied hastily with his request but when he showed displeasure over my not looking Jewish, there was not much I could do but keep silent. I was wise enough not to ignite his displeasure. I was there for one purpose only and that was to obtain my visitation pass to see my mom. Thank God it was granted. I don't mind to tell you that I was starting to feel ill at ease as I have seen Jewish citizens standing up against the wall who were at the headquarters for questioning. Furthermore, I saw a man with a heavy chair running up and down the stairs. It made no sense to me until later on when Terka explained it to me. The poor man had a heart condition. This was definitely the wrong exercise for him but he was forced to do so on purpose.

With my pass firmly in my hand I left anxiously to walk but two buildings further down to the small city jail. The walk seemed to take forever! To describe my visit is very painful to this day. The emotions felt were overwhelming to say the least. I had been seated at a table in the warden's small apartment where he lived with his wife. Both were Czech and under orders from the Gestapo how and what to do. The warden went to get my mom. He held the keys in his hand with which he shortly thereafter unlocked the door of the cell she was kept in. In the meanwhile I watched through the window, as a tall figure emerged which was slowly crossing towards the end of the courtyard, where I was waiting with great trepidation and a racing heart. I kept saying to myself that any minute now I will fling joyfully into my momma's arms. Yes, yes indeed any second now I will feel her warm embrace and her breath upon my cheeks, feeling loved again and secure, even if only for a short while.

The door finally opened slowly and I cried out, "Maminko!" (Czech for Momma), the precious word I kept thinking of every night since she was forced to leave me.

Having said so, I got up ever so fast and flung into her open arms hearing her say, *"Bože můj, nech me se na Tebe podivat moje drahé dite, jak Ty vypadáš? Řekni me jak se Ti daří? Je Terka k Tobe hodná?"* "Dear God, let me look at you my beloved child, let me see what you look like. Tell me how you are doing? Is Terka good to you?" "Yes, yes Momma, she is kind and I am fine! I call her Aunt Terka, it makes me a little less lonely but tell me Momma, how are you and when are you going to be allowed to come back home to me?" She just shook her head sadly uttering quietly, "I don't know my child. I simply don't know. We must keep praying and hoping. It will happen, you'll see. I am innocent."

As she sat down next to me, we looked intently into each other's eyes and I noticed how very tired she looked. Her eyes showed a twinkle of joy as I pulled out the two sandwiches out of my pocket and handed them to her. She ate one immediately and saved the other for later on. She spoke about the cell life she had to endure and spoke of a young lady in the cell next to her, saying that the Gestapo came for her every night and brought her back very late. The young woman kept on singing sorrowfully to the tune of "Ave Maria" until the dawn came. When our visit ended, neither of us realized that it would be the very last time we would ever be together nor see one another again!

My mom was jailed in Vsetin for three weeks, then transferred to Brunn which was the capital of Moravia. From there, after six weeks of incarceration, she was transferred to the first women's concentration camp Ravensbrück in Mecklenburg, Germany. Pain and major disappointment followed for both of us.

Infrequent letters followed and they remained our source of comfort for a long time to come. One entire year went by, including my eleventh birthday. Then one day a letter arrived from mom, with a stamp indicating that it was mailed from Prague.

The letter had informed me of my mom's presence in a Jewish hospital in Prague and of her illness, mainly tuberculosis which she had gotten in Ravensbrück. I was overjoyed and saddened all at the same time. She wrote that she was going to call me at the telegraph office in the village I have lived in on a certain day and at a precise time. You see, phones were scarce and we had none. When the given day arrived I rushed eagerly to the telegraph office and holding my breath, awaited early and impatiently for the phone to ring. When it did, I felt my heart start racing and my hand trembling as I slowly picked up the receiver. I uttered a weak hello and upon hearing my mother's voice, broke into tears and suddenly cried out "MAMINKO!" I heard her strained voice saying to me how much she missed me and wondered if I had plenty to eat and warm clothes to wear. She asked about my progress in school. I asked her when she was coming home. There was a hesitation in her voice. She finally told me about her illness being contagious and informed me that we have to be courageous and sensible for a while longer and postpone our being together until she gets better. My heart sank with disappointment but we both had hope. Little did we realize then that it was not going to happen. We wrote to each other often and I sent her packages with food Terka and friends obtained for her on the black market. You see, there was a food and coal shortage for fuel. People in those days had been rationed with food stamps. We never spoke by phone again. That would have been a great luxury indeed. I sent her photos and she sent one to me. Although it got lost years later, her image on that photo is forever embedded in my mind and heart. I could see that she had suffered, I was a very astute, young in years only, child. I would do some embroidery and send it to her and sometimes crocheted fancy borders on hankies for her. I wanted so to bring her some joy, all along hoping that I will get to see her soon.

In the meanwhile, I kept going to school until one day I had received my report card stamped with the word *"Israelite,"* not permitted to further studies. What a bomb that was for me and another Jewish child by the name of Kurt Bander. All the other children in my school were Christian. During those days I also had to start wearing the *Star of David* on my clothes which spelled out the word "*Jude*," the German word for "*Jew*." I was not allowed to ride the train nor go to certain places but I still could enjoy my bike and that I did. No more formal education, no more piano lessons. The situation in my country started to intensify, still the doctors who took care of my mom tried to bring us together and applied for a travel permit for me under one condition. My mom and I would have to refrain from hugging and kissing when together. Wow! What a promise for a mother and child to keep after a year and a half of separation from each other.

However, fate dealt a cruel blow to me when one day a letter arrived from Prague addressed to Terka, informing her of my mother's death on February 27, 1942 and asking her to be gentle when informing me of my great loss. She was spared from doing so. Unbeknownst to her, I stood in back of her reading the same letter over her shoulder while she was sitting down trying to focus on its content. Whether it was the shock which I had experienced or whether it was a coincidence, who knows, but later on that day I saw blood trickling down my leg as I descended from the stairs and started to scream all over again. I had not realized that on the day I learned of the loss of my mother, I would become a young lady and start to menstruate. I was not prepared; no one told me and I did not know much about one's bodily performance or sex. After all, it was only two months after my eleventh birthday!

Soon after mom succumbed to her illness, I received orders by the German court to leave for Prague where I was placed into a Jewish orphanage. It jarred my entire body, as with my mom gone, I hardly had a reason for wanting to travel to Prague and leave my friends and the place where I was happy. The only good thing about being in Prague was that once again I was able to go to school. It was for Jewish children only. I tried to make new friends and visited my mom's grave at the cemetery every weekend. Her grave still fresh, with nothing planted on it. Is this real? Can this really be true? Is my mother, whom I have longed to see for such a long time underneath this pile of somewhat hardened earth? How could it be? Only three weeks ago she was alive and in this city, but I was not! I was not even allowed or able to come to her funeral. It was not supposed to happen this way, it just was not fair! Isn't life supposed to be fair? I suppose not, what a bitter pill to swallow for a young child like me. Yes, I felt self-pity for both of us and how!

Thoughts in my head were getting crowded as I reminded myself of what went on back home in the village I had lived in and loved. I started to recall the persecution of various citizens and the escalation of arrests geared towards the Jewish citizens whose stores had long been confiscated and replaced with signs of pure "Aryan" establishment.

My thoughts were drifting far away to a city my mother's favorite cousin lived in, whom I saw often and was very close with. I had started to remember a sudden adventure of a few months ago, when I felt so very lonely and was in need of some stroking. Daring as I was, I had suddenly embarked on a short journey to a place called "Moravska Ostrava" where my mom's cousin Erna lived. I did not dare to reveal my sudden plan to "Aunt Terka," fearing that she would try to stop me. I was determined to go and sneaked out, leaving a note behind so she would not worry, saying that I would be back in one or no more than two days. Leaving for the train station, I left the *Star of David* I was to have worn at home. Having purchased a ticket with money which was gifted to me from my uncle in America, off I went. I have visited Moravska Ostrava with my parents often, so I knew my way.

Excited and proud of my accomplishment, I finally stood in front of the apartment where Aunt Erna lived and rang the doorbell. At first there was silence, so I rang again, this time pressing harder, thus the sound of the bell became louder. The door opened slowly and with caution. I spotted Aunt Erna's startled face, staring at me in disbelief. Stunned as she was, I could not tell if she was pleased to see me. When she recovered from her shock, she pulled me quickly inside the door and closed it promptly.

After a quick hug she asked me in a low voice, *"Pro Pána Boha Ilsinko, co Ty tady déláš? Jak jsi se ke mé dostala?"* I could sense that she was very uptight as she spoke these words. "For God's sake, Ilsinko, what are you doing here? How did you manage to get here?" So I told her everything word by word. She was amazed by my innocence and courage. "Come

Ilsinko and have something to eat, you must be hungry, sit down right here. I'll have a plate of soup for you and some bread to eat. Just give me five minutes to warm it up for you. You can have hot chocolate and some cookies too if you want to but then you have to leave. You must understand that you are putting me and yourself in danger." No, that I did not want to hear, not just now. Though hungry and cold, my appetite lessened when I realized I had to leave so soon. There was no way that I could persuade Aunt Erna to let me stay longer. I was crushed as I have looked for some solace and tender nurturing but got none! From her point of view she made the right decision, the only one she could have made under the circumstance, having her husband presently imprisoned in Dachau, Germany. So disappointed and unfulfilled as I was, I left her apartment in less than two hours and went back home, such as it was.

I have remembered this brief encounter in Ostrava and throughout the later years I have never, ever felt close to Aunt Erna again, though I have always wished her well.

Past Reflection And Anticipation

The train was rolling slowly from my hometown to Prague. The journey took almost five hours. In the meantime I tried to read a book but could not concentrate. So I gazed mostly out of the window staring at the wide open fields filled with wild flowers such as daisies, buttercups, blue bells, and my favorite, poppies. Far in the distance were peaks of mountain ranges connecting all around and when I looked up I noticed the pure blue of the sky with hardly any clouds to be seen. I wondered where in that wide horizon was my mom's soul resting or floating at this time.

Wherever she was I knew that she could see me. I could feel her presence.

I started to feel my eyelids getting heavy and allowed myself to doze off. Waking up an hour and a half later, I felt hungry and delved into the food Aunt Terka lovingly prepared for me. I had cold meat loaf, potato salad, roll and later cookies and chocolate milk. Boy, what a treat!

Soon after, my mind started to get active again as I experienced a flashback of when my mom was home and the Czech police came to the door saying, "Mrs. Eichner, we come under the orders of the German government to pick up the gold jewelry and any precious stones that you were notified earlier last week to get ready for us. You may keep your gold wedding ring only. The package with this context will be sealed and kept securely in the bank in Prague. You will receive a receipt. We also need to fingerprint you and your daughter as well. So let's get going. Follow us please." I remembered how very embarrassed I was as my mom advised me that all criminals or otherwise undesirable people had to get fingerprinted. She further told me that we were considered undesirable since we were Jewish. I simply did not get it, not at all!

A couple of weeks later when all was quiet and it seemed safe, my mom went to the window and there on the window sill sat a box made out of plywood filled with sand and cactus plants. I saw her dig underneath and pull out some shiny objects of various sizes. She glanced back at me holding some jewelry up with her hand saying, "Ilsinko, not a word about this to anyone. Do you understand? This is serious stuff, we were lucky to pull this off."

Wow, what experiences I had in my young life to witness, I thought to myself, while wondering what else I might encounter in the days ahead.

I glanced at my watch and just then the conductor came walking into the car and announcing that we will be arriving in Prague in 30 minutes. I stiffend for a while and then looked around at my modest belongings. I put the comb through my hair and said a quick goodbye to the world and life I had known up until now. I sighed deeply as I wondered about my future and the life in the orphanage. The train whistled followed by a screeching sound of the locomotive. Shortly thereafter the conductor asked us to get off, for we now have reached the city of Prague.

As I get off the train with my suitcases someone helped me with and started to look around, I noticed a very tall woman dressed in a dark suit wearing a large hat. She took a few steps towards me and in a pleasant voice said to me, **"You must be Ilsinka Eichnerova, right?"** I nodded my head looking straight into her eyes and said, **"Are you Miss Weingarten?"** "Indeed I am. I came to welcome you and bring you to the orphanage. The girls and boys know about you and are anxious to meet you. We have a very nice group of children there. They are friendly and helpful. You will see. Come my child, give me your hand. Someone will bring the luggage along. Prague is a beautiful city, sometimes referred to as the golden city or golden Prague. You will find out for yourself soon enough. The most important thing is that here you will be able to go to school. It is a Jewish school and we are so happy to have one here. Are you hungry? Dinner will be served in two hours."

When we arrived on Belgicka Ulice Cislo 25 na Kralovskych Vinohradech where the Jewish orphanage was, we were met by Miss Beck and several curious children. From here on, a new experience began.

Soon after, since I needed to wash up, I was shown to my dorm room shared by many other girls more or less of my age. At first I felt a little uncomfortable. However, since I was greeted warmly by everyone, this feeling soon vanished. I was given an orientation and house rules and started to make friends a week later which was not too difficult for me as I had an outgoing nature and a warm smile for everyone. I drew people towards me, having started a new chapter in my life. I made it a practice to continue with my evening prayers, always before bedtime but I also talked to God during the day and wrote down my feelings and happenings around me into a diary which was nothing fancy, more like a plain notebook. So I have decided to draw and color a floral border on the front page, giving the notebook some distinction.

My diary was my confidant and friend, bringing me comfort, laughter, sadness and tears. The last entry I made was about two weeks before having been deported to Terezin where other Jews from Germany, Austria, Holland, and Denmark were deported to. I was kept there for two years from mid October 1942 to mid October 1944. Having survived the deadly Typhus epidemic in Terezin, I found myself in a transport for the second time, this time heading to Auschwitz. My diary however, was safe in the hands of my Christian friends the Lukášes in my hometown where I have sent it before my departure.

3

EICHNERová Ilsa   bez.

21.12.1929   /mojž./

Praha

VS   VSETÍN.

na Plavisku 1111

ÚSTŘEDNÍ KARTOTÉKA — TRANSPORTY.

R. č. _49.556_

Eichnerová Ilsa

Rodná data: _21.12.1929_

Adresa před deportací: _XV., Belgická 35_

HLASEN
oo
EVIDENCE

1. transport	2. transport
dne: 24.X.1942	dne: 18.X.944
	číslo: Eš 1016
Ca č.61f	Osvětim

I.

Deportation Orders

THE DIARY

(Written by Ilsinka (Ilse) Eichnerova and translated in the USA by the author from her native Czech).

Můj životopis!!

Narodila jsem se 21. XII. 1929 ve Vsetíně. Žila jsem tam s rodiči 10 let a měla jsem se tam dobře. Měla jsem hodně kamarádek a velkou zahradu, kde jsem si vždycky s dětmi hrála a nebo jsem šla s mamičkou na procházku.

Potom jsme se odstěhovali do Růžďky, do jedné vesnice která byla od Vsetína vzdálena vlakem jen 1/4 hod. Bylo tam krásně.

Dear Diary:

I was born on 12-21-1929 in Vsetin, Czechoslovakia. I lived there with my parents for 9 years and I had a very good life. I had a great many girlfriends and a big garden where we all played. If I did not do that, I would go for walks with my mom. Later on we moved to a nearby village of Ruzdka which could be reached by train in less than a half hour. It was so beautiful there.

Mom

I lived there with my mom. Then the day arrived when my mom had to take leave of me and I had to remain behind while a woman whom I hardly knew came to look after me. At first we had a hard time getting along but later on we became accustomed to one another. We would often go to the woods together to look for pine cones. We also climbed up the hills and looked down with the help of binoculars in the direction of the train station, waiting, hoping that we would spot my mom walking out of there. In fact, one day last week we had waited until 9:30 p.m., watching for every incoming train. Not only didn't my mom come back to me but she was taken even further from me, to the city of Brno, and approximately three months later, she was sent far, far away, to Ravensbruck, in Germany. This was in the year of 1940. It was first on July 6, 1941 that she finally came back to our country to the city of Prague. We were separated for two long years altogether.

This year was very cruel to me. I have lost my mom for good. My beloved, ever so good mom died after a lengthy illness on February 27, 1942. I think that she was buried on March 4th. I could not attend because I was living in Ruzdka and had to stay. Oh I was so sad. At this time I was calling the woman who was taking care of me, Aunt Terka. Three weeks after mom's death, I was sent to Prague to the orphanage, against my will of course. I was incredibly unhappy. I was picturing the orphanage differently but actually it is nice here and I like it a lot. Mainly I am able to go to school here and all the children are so very nice. Nevertheless I long for Ruzdka, the fields full of wildflowers, the woods that I used to go to and the people I cared for. It is two months since I got here. How quickly the time goes by. Before long, school will be over. Boy, do I ever look forward to my summer freedom. No homework then.

A child was orphaned at the age of 11. To remember that day is painful. "My one and only beloved mom, I will never forget you. The weeds will never overtake the path to your grave, ever. It simply must not happen."

Partial view of castle in Vsetin
My beloved fatherland, the Czech wide open fields everywhere
how I love you, Oh how I love you!!!

Ty moje otcino, Vy ceska lada, ma duse ma Vas tak rada, ach
rada!!!

My motto is: **May freedom prevail everywhere!**

Friday, May 22, 1942

Nothing new to report. Yesterday was the last day for all of us. We are off because of the holidays. We went swimming and then performed various chores. We sure have enough of those to do. By the way, those children whose marks were low and who have a parent will get a report card sent home to them.

On Tuesday, we had to write a composition as it is a monthly assignment. We had to do one for our German class, Czech class, and for Geography as well. I don't know what my grades are as yet, but the German teacher forewarned us that our compositions as a whole were lousy.

Saturday, May 23, 1942

It was raining yesterday and we were worried that the weather may not hold out. So we prayed yesterday for good weather to come. In the morning we experienced some dampness but later on it all cleared up. It was truly a lovely Saturday. I cleaned up the study room after lunch, put on a playsuit and went out on the balcony. Other girls were there too, mainly, Ilse, Hanuse, Ilsinka, and Cinda. We were busy tanning ourselves and smeared some Vaseline all over our bodies as the sun was too hot. Then we started to argue. We tired of it shortly and soon thereafter left for the courtyard.

We sat on the swings, and afterwards had a snack and played volleyball. Linda was not careful, she somehow, I don't know how it happened, ended up with a bruise on her nose while trying to hit the ball and at the same time twisted her foot. Wham! She got very startled and two taller and older girls came to her rescue. Her foot was hurting so that she was unable to walk by herself. I accompanied her to the doctor who strapped her foot and ankle which helped her a lot. I assisted her when she had to go up and down the stairs. Once again we returned to the courtyard and laid down in lounging chairs. The doctor who fixed Linda's foot was sitting next to us. (I have nicknamed him Trumbum on Spachtle). It just came to me suddenly. This silly name had no particular meaning yet the mere sound of it made me laugh and Linda too. We laughed, stopped and started all over again till the tears swelled up our eyes. Gosh, that was just the greatest, the laugher I mean. I simply could not stop. I have not laughed in a long, long time. At 6:30, dinner was served. We had spinach and potatoes. I am sitting presently on the balcony writing to you, my Diary, while thinking about all the dear people in Ruzdka I had to leave behind.

Well, I will go now to the gym and exercise a bit which will perk me up. Afterwards I will wash up and go to sleep. While I was thinking that, Rose and Ilsinka were also sitting on the balcony, so I have asked them to accompanying me. It was slowly getting dark. The gym had several windows facing the courtyard. Miss Beckova was there playing volleyball. We had to be careful that she should not see us. Suddenly we heard some odd sounds which started to grow louder as they got closer. Quickly, we decided to go to hide. After a while I gave myself some courage to peek out and see who was around there. I barely took a step forward when I spotted Hans standing in front of me. I got so startled that my foot slipped and I almost fell. I gave out a scream. Hearing that, Miss Beckova, whom I referred to as "Becka" came to the gym. When she saw us there she started to get excited. Hans made a quick getaway. I pretended to be looking for some clothing in the locker. She spoke to Rose and forbid her to go to the courtyard and as for Ilsinka, well she did not find her. She hid at first and then ran off. How lucky can you be?

Sunday, May 24, 1942

We got up late and after breakfast immediately put on tops and shorts as it was quite warm. We went out into the court. The girls were teaching me how to play throw and catch, as well as volleyball. We played the entire afternoon. It was swell. We washed before going to lunch. Afterwards I went to visit my aunt who lives in Flora. Polda (my cousin) was not allowed. Everyone from his room was punished because the boys screamed during the night. So they were not allowed to go visit over the holidays. Therefore I went by myself. I went with my aunt to the park. It sure was beautiful out there. When it came time to go home my cousin said to me, "Take the Koruni Street till you come to the church of Saint Ludmila on Kingdom Square." I said fine, but decided to try to shorten my trip. So I made a turn on another street and got lost. I started to have fear over how I will get back home. I am still not too familiar here with what is where and how to find my way. I wandered around for approximately twenty minutes before coming upon the tracks where the number three streetcar runs. From that landmark on, I knew already how to get back.

Monday, May 25, 1942

I went with Polda to our aunt and then to the Olsanske Cemetery to visit my mother's grave and also the grave of Mr. Sax. We stayed there for quite some time. Afterwards we left for Hagibor. I like it there. The sun was shining brightly. We met there several girls from the orphanage including Marianna. Polda decided to stay longer, so Marianna and I decided to walk back slowly to the orphanage. Since it was hot, we took off our coats.

Tuesday, May 26, 1942

Well, the holidays are over and we have to go back to school today.

Wednesday, May 27, 1942

Yesterday my tonsils swelled again so I stayed put in bed. Today I feel simply perfect again. It sure hurt yesterday, even this morning but now the pain is gone.

My German composition turned out real bad. I got an "F." I don't know how I did so lousy. I will have to improve, that's for sure. We think that the school year will end by July 15th, it is not certain as yet. That is surely dumb. Nobody will care to study during the hot summer month; the report cards will be a bust.

I received a letter from "Aunt" Terka this afternoon. It always brings me such joy.

Thursday, May 29, 1942

REMEMBERING.

Today it is already three months since my beloved mom is gone. Not so long ago she was still here with the rest of us but to me it seems like an eternity.

My dear momma,

I beg you most sincerely to protect me and to somehow look after me. Should I be doing something that is wrong, something that is not right to do, send some intuition my way, so that I can correct it. Momma, I want and hope that I will succeed in being a good daughter, so that you could get some joy from that. I know that you are watching from above. I want you to feel pride in me, mainly you my beloved momma, for you had so little joy, and also Aunt Terka!

Friday, May 29, 1942

Yesterday was very hot. I simply could not stand it in bed, so I sat on the windowsill and was tanning myself in the sun.

The evening was still full of humidity. I kept splashing myself with cold water. We kept the window open and Helga and I kept staring at the sky, which was full of heavy clouds. The spring air is laced with the scent of that season.

Suddenly a fairly large plane appeared above, with a green light reflecting. We kept watching till it disappeared from sight.

Shortly after we spotted three more airplanes, smaller ones and well lit. The sight of them was very pleasing to me. Finally we went to sleep. By then it was 10:30 p.m. already.

It is thundering.

The weather is not the greatest, it is raining and I am laid up. Doctor "Hurvinek" already made his rounds to the infirmary. He said that I am coming along and will be able to get up before long. I have had visitors. Betty and Lanka, but I am still bored here, I don't care to be in bed. I like to be among the rest of the girls and would much prefer to go to school rather than being laid up lazing around while other children are playing in the yard.

Saturday, May 30, 1942

It is already 7:00 in the evening. We had knockwurst for dinner. I did some reading in the afternoon. For lunch I had some beef broth and mashed potatoes. I studied some, then got up to stretch a little. I simply could not stand it in bed any more. I started to mend socks. It is almost evening now and the sun is setting. I will wash up and go to bed again. There is no sleep in me. I am praying and as I am doing so, various memories are hauntingly going through my head.

Tuesday, June 2, 1942

I am well again. I was in school today. Yesterday I was still home, so in the morning after breakfast Ilsinka and I had dining room duty, which meant clearing the cups from the tables, wiping them thoroughly and sweeping the floor. We came upstairs at 9:00 a.m. Then I went with Claudia to the photographer. By then it was noontime. I went to set the tables for lunch.

In the afternoon Lianka and I went to straighten out our belongings in the closet. Then I went with Irene Roubiczek to buy a bow for Georgie's violin. Came back at 4:30 p.m. and had a snack and went into the kitchen to help clean the spinach. There was lots of it. The other helpers who were there were Brauska, Jula, Fini, Liana, Margit, Lia, Karel Eisner, Peter Frank and myself. Betty came later on in the day. For dinner that evening were boiled potatoes with the skin, so we were busy peeling them. On the whole, the day passed pleasantly.

The Girls from the Orphanage
(LIANA wearing kerchief left side, CINDA w/flowers in hair
second from the right side).

However, there was an incident which made me very sad. Honza was thrown out of the kitchen. That did not bother me as much as the fact that Honza is no longer wanted in the orphanage. The decision will be made by Sunday, I think. I am praying that all should end well. Betty and Fini will try to put in a good word for him. That would be truly awful, if he had to leave. He does not even have anywhere to go. He got into something bad, for the madam (orphanage director for the boy's division) herself threw him out.

Besides the kitchen incident, he also got into trouble with Pick. Boys are not allowed in the closet but he went anyway and the teacher, Mr. Pick saw him there and slapped his face. Honza did likewise to the teacher. Oh boy, that was a bad move on his part. (Well, there is more to it. Something else happened which I don't know about). So, all I can do is hope for the best. When I think of Honza, I feel sad.

When I went to school I thought of him instead of paying attention to my work. We were going over correcting the Czek composition and were graded for spelling, sentence structure and style. I got 100 for composition, 65 for spelling and for sentence structure 80. I did not really have lots of mistakes, only about four, but boom, down goes the mark, big time. That is really not fair. We have a very strict teacher. Today we decided to elect leaders among ourselves and hold an election for the office of the president (which went to Kopelovic) and his assistant is Bohmova.

Saturday, June 6, 1942

Yesterday was an incredibly crazy day. When we woke up at 7:00, Mrs. Ungelaider walked in informing us that Annalies, Pipca and Lili received notice that they were being summoned for transport. Annalies was just recuperating from an operation of 14 days ago and could not manage to take care of things. At the news, we all jumped out of bed instantly. Fortunately we had no school yesterday and so we energetically got going mending stockings, fixing underwear, washing whatever was needed. All of us pitched in to do something for her. All three girls were all packed when the telephone rang from the Jewish Federation stating that they should not go yet, to report that they are in a reserve and that in all probability they will not be transported as of yet. However, they had to remain in a state of readiness. I gave Annalies a little chain necklace as a remembrance of me. She was happy.

Today's noon meal consisted of noodle soup, potatoes, meatloaf and a green salad. After lunch I cleaned up the study room and later on wrote letters. When I finished, I went to buy stamps. Thereafter the girls were begging me to go to "Belehradska Ulice" for some ice cream. I could not find an ice cream store but was determine to keep on looking for one. Honza also asked me to get him some and gave me a cup to fill up. If I did not come back with some ice cream, he would have called me "chicken," "scaredy-cat" and the girls as well. So I went down "Manes Street" and sure enough there was a store where I got plenty of ice cream. By the time I got back home it was 5:30 p.m. already. I was looking for an ice cream store up and down the streets for 1½ hours, taking chances by not wearing the *Star of David*, identifying me as a Jew. Wearing it would have made it impossible for me to enter the store and buy the ice cream. So yes, I took my chances, more than once.

Evening for dinner we had kielbasa with mustard, some bread and sugar cubes. Afterwards I was with Lianka in our dressing room looking out the window. Honza was a flight above us and spit on us (that pig!). We walked away and went to bed. Margit, who looks a bit like my Aunt Adele, crept into the bed with me and we kept horsing around and finally started to fight, after which she left. All of us were ready by then to go to sleep except for Hanuse and Irene. They were still sitting on the windowsill and kept kidding around. Hanuse always likes to look at the stars, wonders which one is Dzeryk and is she still remembered. Hanka is an incredibly lively girl.

Sunday, June 7, 1942

I studied this morning and I put on a new dress after lunch as I was going to my aunt's. Miss Beckova came over to me asking, "Do you have homework?" I replied, "No, not really! I will come home a little earlier tonight and do it then." Miss Beckova did not allow me to leave. I had to sit down and do my homework first. It really was not much at all. I was finished in half an hour. Then left with Trixie. We bought ice cream for 5k (Kronen) and went to the old Jewish cemetery on "Ziskov." The cemetery was closed. So we went on to my aunt in Flora. Trixie accompanied me. We sat in the courtyard, had a snack and went on home. We had so much fun going back, walking passed the Rieger Park and gardens, kidding, laughing, even kissing. At the same time she pretended that I was Otta and I was going to pretend that she was Honza but by that time we had reached our home. So I did not get to act my part out. Oh well, it was already 6:00 p.m.

Monday, June 8, 1942

We had school this morning but since our teacher had to leave earlier today, we got to go home an hour sooner. I had homework to do this afternoon, then suddenly Miss Weingarten, the orphanage director for the girl's division, appeared saying that we had to go to help out and do our duty at the Federation. So I got dressed quickly and left with Cinda to go there. We were given five addresses in Králové Vinohrady as well as in "Ziskov." We took care of what we had to at three of the places but did not get to the two other ones. We kept looking for approximately two hours for the other two addresses in Varta, without any luck. By then our feet were aching. Cinda said that she has had it for the day. All sorts of confusing instructions were given to us. When we finally got on streetcar number 7, the conductor told us that we should have taken the number 2 instead. He looked at the handwritten note which was given to us saying that "on Varta," was a street in Libnice, another sector of Prague entirely. I was dismayed and said to Cinda, "Don't you think that we should get off? To this she replied, "Oh please leave me alone." A while later the conductor came to us again asking where we were heading for. Cinda looking out discovered that by now we were in the vicinity of The Olshanske Cemetery. Well we laughed it off and got out of the streetcar and into another. We headed back to the Federation but not before having collected a bunch of tickets from the streetcar. We ended up with 73 which came to 21k (Kronen). We were originally given only 20k car fare. We have spent 12k so were left with 8. For the errands we did, we each were given 10k. Afterwards we headed for home. By that time it was half past seven. Along the way, we met Mr. Otta Schon. He used to live in my hometown. He invited me to come to see him and the rest of the family.

That evening we had potatoes, spinach and 1 kohlrabi for dinner. I laid down later on Irene's bed next to Hana, as Irene was under the weather and spent the night in the infirmary. It is getting dark outside but the sky is beautiful and blue as a forget-me-not. In the still of the evening one can hear the sound of the plane circling over Prague. I look out. The window is open and the warm fresh air is filtering in. In the room next to us where the older girls are resting a sound of laughter is coming through and the conversation is growing louder. The light is out by now in our bedroom. Next to me lies Hana sound asleep by now, while I am saying my prayers. The voices heard in our bedroom are getting fewer, as one girl after another is nodding off to sleep, uttering softly good night.

Tuesday, June 9, 1942

Ilsinka and I had dining room duty. It was precisely 11:45 a.m. when Miss Weingarten came in to tell me that my aunt phoned saying the she needs me and wants me very much, as her daughter Editka has died. I ate my lunch rapidly, took my school case along with me and off I went to "Kelleyova Street." My aunt is terribly distraught. She has not seen her daughter in 3¼ years. (Her name was Edith, we called her "Dita." *She was arrested as a student in Prague walking with other students. When they encountered young German soldiers in the street they spit in front of them. They were arrested and Dita being Jewish, was sent to the concentration camp Ravensbruck in Germany, where my mom was as well. That was where Dita died).*

We learned little in school today. We were studying geography and I paid very little attention. I was in a very peculiar mood and acted silly. I kept sending notes to Ilsinka and she sent some back to me. The messages were intended to be funny but in truth, they were stupid. In spite of it we had to laugh.

Wednesday, June 10, 1942

Nothing much happened during the day. From school I went directly to my aunt to the hospital where she worked. I returned home at 3:45 p.m. and had something to eat. It was puree of peas. Then I went back to my aunt. I had snacks at her place. Sat down for a while and did some knitting. Afterwards she and I went to visit some of her acquaintances. I had some derma and bread with butter. I did not feel hungry. I must have overeaten earlier. We had knockwurst for dinner, bread and salad. An hour later I felt hungry. Later that evening we had to mend our clothing and we got a danish and tea. It was meant for Annalies to take along but since she did not leave, we got to eat it instead.

Thursday, June 12, 1942

Today we got a new teacher. He is young and has blond hair. I think that he will be fun to be with. Till now we had our principal Roubiczek. We are presently learning how to figure percentages. In the afternoon Ilsinka and I had to do some preparing for the next class. We wanted to go afterwards to the cemetery but we could not. We were asked again to be on duty and go to see different people in Vinohradech and Ziskov. We managed to buy ourselves some ice cream. After that, we went to my aunt who lives in Flora, since we were not too far from there. At least we ate well there. Then we continued on to the Premyslova Street and stopped by a lady's house who spoke no Czek. So I started to speak to her in German. As soon as I started to say anything, she started to interrupt. So after a few minutes she and I got all mixed up. Ilsinka started to speak to her slowly in Czek. She was telling her that the lady was the first one to request our services through the Jewish Federation. Then the lady repeated again in German that she did not understand Czek. In turn, Ilsinka did not understand German. Ilsinka thought that the lady said the she was pleased to be the first one. Since I understood her, I had a good laugh as the lady said no such thing. Whenever two of us go on duty in order to perform some good deeds, there is fun. We got some cookies and 7k and got home around 8:00 p.m. We had for dinner potatoes in the skin, salad, a small piece of butter and raw kohlrabi. Afterwards all of us had to sew patches on clothing. We also drank tea and had a danish. We took it back from Annalise since she did not have to leave. We had packed it originally for her trip. So we all had a piece now in celebration of her staying. The poor thing was summoned today again.

I am resting next to Lianka. I like her a lot. Last night when we were lying down, Liana read to me from the collection by Jiri Wolker. In the morning we took a bath together and I helped her get ready. We did our homework. For lunch we had a casserole. Then I took a ride to the Jewish Federation to bring back a riding permit for Miss Weingarten. I rode along the riverfront, looking at the Vltava River seeing wild ducks in the water and small boats floating gracefully by. Looking up, there in the background was the picturesque panorama of the Hradczin castle. Today the water of the Vitava looked muddy. The riverfront so far is the nicest place I have seen in all of Prague.

Sunday, June 14, 1942

I went today to Aunt Jenny's for lunch. It was delicious. Beef soup with chunks of meat and noodles, potatoes with "griebene," thick hamburger-meatloaf patty, a tort and a bun. Then I went with my aunt to the Blochs. Dear Diary, you do not know them, right? Doctor Bloch was taking care of my momma while she was ill and was very nice to her. Today is just one month since he got married to Marticka. She is not registered with him and now she alone received a summons to report for transport. He went voluntarily and requested that he be taken also. That is why we went over to help them pack, sew a few things and do whatever else was needed. Then we went to get some ice cream and stopped for a second at my aunt's friends where we had some sweet rolls. Afterwards back again to the Blochs. This was only the second time that I have ever seen Marticka. I like her very much. She is pretty and very kind. She is good and though only nineteen years old, very courageous and independent. She is not afraid of anything, even though she knows that it might cost her life. She is heroic and keeps on saying that perhaps she will hold out after all. She gave me a lot of her belongings. Tomorrow at 9:00 in the morning, both of them are to report. We were saying are goodbyes today. As I left for home, I kept seeing them before my eyes. I can not begin to tell you, my Dear Diary, how badly I have felt. I cried all the way home feeling very sad. It is awful, dear God, so awful! They were allowed to take with them only 50kg and even that they will not let them keep. What a pity. Poor Marticka and her husband too! How pitiful for all of those who had to leave already. Just at this time while sitting here making entries in my Diary, I recalled Camilla, Dasa, Dzeryk a Smudla, wondering what they are doing now. Soon I will have to include Annalise, Pipca and Lila Newman in my memories, for these three dear girls are regretfully also leaving for the unknown. Who knows how they are going to have to live. I am sure that they will think of us here at the orphanage with fond memories.

Diary, my pal that you are to me, I am in a very peculiar mood today. Yes, I am also sad. The transports keep coming up and they are getting to me, so much so that I wish I could be back in my old home. I like it here in the orphanage and don't mind being here except for Sundays and vacations, that's when I would like to be back in Ruzdka again.

Monday, June 15, 1942

I came home at 2:00 p.m. We had some kind of goulash, made mostly out of potatoes. Then I went to visit Mrs. Silberman where I was trying on some dresses. After that I had to take a German dictation as my homework assignment. Gosh I misspell a lot.

The weather today is miserable and it is raining. I am sitting in the study hall, looking out occasionally. I spotted some underwear spread out on one table and kids studying next to one another. The younger children are in the playroom and are behaving themselves. Well, at least it is quiet here. As a rule the younger ones are scrapping around and fighting with one another. Peter is playing the harmonica and the piano too. I am copying the arithmetic assignment from Ilsinka. Then I will go to move my things into Annalies' locker, as mine is smaller and the one she has been using is so much better.

Monday evening. At about 8:45 p.m. the door suddenly opened and there stood Lili and Kopelovic. We thought that we were dreaming or something but soon found out that what we were seeing and hearing was not a dream but reality. I was in our sleeping quarters at that time where Lianka and I were getting ready for bed, when we heard them say, "Girls, Annalies and Pipca came back again." We did not believe it for a minute but when they insisted that it really was the truth, we went out to look. Lisa and Lili were surrounded by children screaming with joy never-ending. They too have returned. We moved out of our bedroom into the hall. Miss Weingarten and the director of the boys' quarters came running down the staircase and hugged Mr. Cenkra, who brought the girls back. There was so much excitement going on. When Honza saw Lisa, he ran quickly to tell the boys. The boys could not care less that they were not allowed on our floor and into our quarters. They jumped out of their beds and came down as they were, mostly in pajamas, to greet and hug the children who have just returned. Lisa was so thrilled and Pipca too. Lila went to sleep, she was tired and felt weak from all that she had experienced earlier. The eyes of Kopelovic were radiant with joy. Prior to noon when the children had to take leave from us to enter the centrum from which they were to be deported, he was so sad and everyone was crying. In the evening upon their return they were totally different kids. We all rejoiced with them. After having greeted all the children one by one, we took Lisa into our bedroom and listened eagerly to her saga. It was quite late by the time we finished talking and went to sleep.

Tuesday, June 17, 1942

We aired out our bedding in the morning and after breakfast, cleaned up the dining hall. Then we concentrated on our homework. Prior to noontime, we had to hurry and set the tables. (We had soup and big dumplings with a tomato sauce). Then we went to grab our permits and took the streetcar to school. Boy, did we have fun. We got new classmates as of seven days ago. They are fun to be with. We kept laughing the entire afternoon, aggravating the teachers. We did not go home directly after school. We went to Ilsinka's mom and had something to eat first, afterwards took the rail home. After dinner we were handing out fresh underwear and tee shirts for everyone. Then Lana and I went to wash our socks. With luck we had warm water, so we were also able to take a bath. I was telling jokes and kidding around and both of us kept laughing. Finally we said goodnight and went to sleep.

Saturday, June 20, 1942

Lianka and I bathed this morning and then spent the rest of the morning grinding over our German assignment. Yesterday a package came from Aunt Adele full of goodies.

My Diary! The day before brought me such joy. I received a letter from Drazka followed by a photo postcard from her sister Maria depicting the house in Ruzdka I used to live in. Before that I kept crying thinking about my momma. I felt sorry for myself because others had a mom and I did not. Just then Miss Weingarten walked in with the postcard photo of the house. It made me so very happy, I stopped crying. Also, Lianka came over to me to comfort me, saying that not everybody has a mom and that I should come with her. So I followed her to Erna who was playing the piano, while Eva and Trixi were singing. Afterwards I left with Lianka to straighten out our closets. I like Lilianka the best of all. She is such a dear, kind kid. After her comes Cinda. Yes, I like her a lot too, but Lianka comes first. I have nicknamed both of them. I call Lianka Strap, Cinda is Cvok and I am Spunt.

Photo of the house in Ruzdka where my mother was taken away from

Monday, June 22, 1942

This was the last home I had with my mother. Next to it was the post office building with an apartment above where a former retired mayor lived. From there you could see the Becva River, where I used to go swimming. To the other side is a hilly sunny area where I used to go picking berries and wild strawberries. They were so delicious, very sweet, and a good size too. In the springtime, I used to go there and plant tiny tree seedlings. Not too far from there were beautiful woods. To the right of the woods was an area where I used to go at times with the former mayor to look for mushrooms. To the left of the woods was a clearing with two nice cottages. One named "At the Wolfs," the other belonging to Mr. Blablo had no special name. There were times when I went with Drazka to take her goat there to graze. Today came a postcard from Drazka with a photograph of the school where I went in my 5th grade. Drazka wrote that she is still picking strawberries and that she is riding her bicycle all the way to the Bystricka Dam. That I truly envy her doing. Here where I live now, strawberries do not grow and I have nowhere to go swimming. That is really dumb. It would be perfect to live here in Prague

73

during the school year, but the rest of the year I would like to be back home where I used to live. It makes me so sad. I would like to be able to travel and go to visit Aunt Terka and sometimes Aunt Adele. Oh well, the truth is that I would like to be there all the time if it was at all possible.

Photo of School in Bystricka

Yesterday noon I had lunch at my aunt's. We had wiener schnitzel. Last Saturday while I was visiting, she gave me fried fish with potatoes, milk, bread and butter, a piece of chocolate and other good stuff. In the afternoon, Erna, Eva and Rose went with me to a meadow, where we stretched out and were sunbathing. Then we had a snack. Later on Rose decided to do some fancy gymnastic exercises. She did real good, for sure.

Monday, June 22, 1942

Today I had bad luck in school. I was told twice to leave the classroom. Once because I was caught eating during class while studying geography. It was only a beef jerky but Miss Helen saw me and I got called out. The second time I had to leave and Ilsinka also, was because of Herman Kuzny. On the "desk" before me a note was placed meant for me. It said, "Dear Milo, I would like to go steady with you, Herman." But he was not the one who wrote it. It was a prank. Ilsinka and I kept laughing over it during our Czek class and we were told to leave the classroom once again. So then Herman picked up the note and afterwards tried to scribble the Morse code on it. A new teacher came into the class and asked Herman to hand the note over to him but he refused and tore it up instead. If he had done that to some other teacher there would have been trouble all right but this new rooky teacher let it ride, he is okay, so far anyway.

Today I received a picture postcard of Ruzdka from Zdenka which said, "Sincere greetings from Konvic from Zdena. Regards from Kristine. Write us *soon*!" I have no time right now to write you a letter but will do so later.

Wednesday, June 24, 1942

School started today at 8:00 a.m. In the first hour we were given a test in home economics. Yesterday we had one in math, religion, and other. On one part of math I got a "B," the other I don't know yet. Religion a "B," geography a "B" also. We had fun during the religious class. By the way, I was all mixed up with dates of events. Knowing that, I took precaution and slipped a dictionary into my desk. I was lucky that Leba did not see me do it. I only hope that he will not test me orally. (Of course, I copied from the dictionary).

Thursday, June 25, 1042

I was excused yesterday afternoon from dining hall duty. Immediately after lunch I went with Fini and Erna to the collection center with our outgrown underwear. Afterwards I went to put on shorts and went to organize our closet. Later on I went out into the yard, sat on a stool and tried to get stains out of my dress. Honza was there laying down and sunning himself. Ferenz and Pick got a hold of a water hose. They hosed down the courtyard and, of course, Honza and the other children as well. There was lots of screaming going on. In the far corner was a large basin and some pails of water so the younger children were there splashing around and wading. The grownups, Lili Muller, wife of the director, her friend Ace, and Carl Eisner were engaged in playing volleyball. Then came dinner. We had tea and sweet rolls. Afterwards Ilsinka and I had to clean up but we had to wait first for the boys to get finished eating. So we remained close to the kitchen which is a good place to be. Brauska gives the boys always seconds and when we hang around, we also end up getting extras. She gave us more tea and two more sweet rolls each. They were good.

This morning Ilsinka and I had to prepare for our Czek lesson. Pretty soon will be lunch time. I heard that we were going to have cherry dumplings. I do have a yearning for them. In the afternoon, back to school.

Miss Beckova whom we nicknamed "Becka" is a dear. She truly is. She looks after us and is right in doing what she is doing even though we don't always like it very much. School began today at shortly after 8:00. I remembered having left my apron in the bedroom last evening, which is not allowed. We are not supposed to leave anything that doesn't belong there. I have simply overlooked putting the apron into my closet drawer. When I returned from school I looked for it everywhere but without any luck. I went upstairs as usual to announce that I was home. I barely put my foot into the door saying, "Hello, Miss Beckova," when I heard her saying to me, "Milco, you are not getting any allowance this week anymore. Here, take your apron. You left it laying around where it didn't belong." Oh boy, no money, just when I was planning on having my picture taken. Becka said that I have spent too much already and that was that! She can be touch sometimes and make my life difficult. I know in my heart that she is right but honestly, she could give one at least 10k. Well, if she won't, I'll go to my aunt, she offered the other day all on her own to pay for my picture but I don't want a photo of me alone. I want to take one with Lianka.

Friday, June 26, 1942

School started today at 9:45 a.m. and ended one hour earlier than usual. I came home and changed my clothing. I put on a red plaid dress and since I had a blouse of the same print I lend it to Ilsinka so that we would look like sisters. We went to Hagibor where we were to participate in some gymnastics but since we came late, we had to watch. Across from Hagibor is the cemetery, so I went over to visit my momma's grave. I no longer saw a pile of dirt but a neatly shaped grave, ready for planting. I brought my momma a small bouquet of daisies, the poor dear. She loved these flowers the best next to violets. From there we ran to catch a streetcar getting back home at 7:00 instead of 6:30 p.m. We were fearful and kept praying that Becka shouldn't be around when we got back. We ran upstairs and bumped into Marianna asking, "Was dinner served already?" I guess she did not pay attention to us because she answered, "Yes, it was!" So now what? We were forced to look for Becka to let her know that we came back late and have not eaten. Ilsinka worried so, that she went clutching a good luck charm. Both of us were trying to imagine what either Becka or Miss Weingarten will say to us. Will Becka say that we will not be allowed to go anywhere on Sundays, or that we are forbidden to go into the garden for the entire week, or will Miss Weingarten say that we will have three days of dining room duty or what? All of these thoughts were buzzing through our little heads. As luck had it, all ended well. Dinner was not over yet. All of them were still in the dining hall and as for Becka and Miss Weingarten, they were not around, neither was Leidka (our nickname for Miss Ungeleider). So all ended well, the lucky charm worked for us this time.

Saturday, June 27, 1942

Nothing special doing. I took a bath and then concentrated hot and heavy on studying German as I was going to take an exam given by Director Roubiczek who was going to determine whether I could be promoted to a higher class. For lunch we got soup, potatoes and hash. Afterwards I had to do the wash. I wanted to get going and planned on visiting my aunt. I walked through the study hall and up to Becka whom I asked if I could leave. She replied, "You are not going to go anywhere just yet! Go get Helga and study your German but first kindly help Rose to get the study hall straightened up. When you finish with that and your homework studies, then you may go." I studied pretty quickly but by the time Becka tested me and I got through with everything else, it was 6:00 p.m. before I got to my aunt's and guess what? She was not home. So I dropped by her friend's house, had a light bite and headed back to the orphanage. I had time to play for a while in the courtyard. Trixi is going steady again with Otta and Cinda, "Cvok" is stuck on Jirka Fisher. Cvok keeps a funny looking monkey in her bed, she pretends that it is Jirka. One time she could not find him. Oh boy, Dear Diary, you should have seen that commotion! She was out of it, carried on so silly. She did not find the monkey until the next day. I had lots of fun tonight. Wherever Lianka went, I went too. I followed her like a little puppy. I tried to hold on to her skirt, stuck my thumb in my mouth acting like a baby.

Afterwards we played hide and seek. I crawled under the bed and when she headed for the door and turned around, she got a glimpse of me partially sticking out. So she grabbed my leg and started to pull. When she got me out I quickly grabbed hers and she fell. By then we had enough of silliness and we laid down onto the bed. My dear, dear Strap, I care for her a lot. I would be so sad without her around. We took photos of both of us together at the photographer's recently. It will take one month before we get the photos back. They cannot have them ready sooner for us so what can we do but patiently wait. We don't know what is ahead! I hope that she will be able to stay here for some time. If they take her and she has to go by herself, I would pity her so much. She would have to leave her mom and sister behind. Dear God that would be so awful. When my time comes to leave, all that I will be leaving behind here will be my momma's grave. My wish is that we both get summoned for the transport at the same time, so that we could remain together. Who knows, it may not happen. Whatever, my mom and God will somehow look after me.

Sunday, June 28, 1942

I went to Zabehlic this afternoon with my cousin Polda. He was showing me a new way of getting there, through two other parts of Prague called Nusle and Michle. Uncle Franta works with Rudi in Karlsberge. He comes home on Sundays but this time he did not. So Aunt Stella and little Vera came to Zabehlic to be with Aunt Ida, Uncle Max and Leosek. We were all together. We had something to eat and they even stuffed our pockets with cookies. Then Aunt Stella asked us to take Verushka out to play. So we did. We remained in front of our house and later on wandered off into a nearby field. Polda and Leosek did not waste any time. They had a long rope that they pulled out of nowhere and one, two, three, they started to wind it around me. I did not know what hit me and of course I could not walk. Those mischief-makers! Finally they let go of me. When I got loose again, I grabbed little Vera and ran away from the boys. We came to walk past someone's garden and looking in we saw various fruits about to ripen. The bushes were loaded with gooseberries and other red currants. We also saw big strawberries peering out from underneath the wide leaves of the strawberry plants. It was half past five when we said goodbye and Polda and I took off for home. We kept walking and by the time we passed Nusle where we had to climb quite a few steps, I wished we had been home already. We ate at our aunt's house big pieces of challah, then cookies and other stuff. Polda started to feel sick. I was not sick yet but almost, and I told Polda that I felt like gagging. He said, "Me too! You know what? Let's race and see who gets home first." I liked that idea and started to run all the way and rushed straight to the toilet. Nothing happened but I somehow felt obliged to tell Polda that I threw up. Too bad, I lied.

Monday, June 29, 1942

Well, we got a newcomer to the orphanage. She is 9 years old and her name is Ritta B. She did not go to school last year. So right after vacation time she will be going to the 4th grade, though actually she should be in 5th grade. I was assigned to look after her. I have to make sure that she gets washed and help her every evening to do it. I also wash her socks. When she gets more used to everything and becomes more outgoing, then she'll do it herself. She is old enough. Still when I was her age, I didn't do this for myself either. My momma did it all but when she was no longer home with me, I had to get going and do it all. When I still had her, she would supervise the bath time, other routine cleanliness I definitely handled myself. So Ritta will slowly get to doing things for herself also. She is from Vienna, speaks German fluently and Czek as well. I played the piano for her and she listened. When Rudy came, we had a musical evening and he taught us two new folk songs. He orchestrated our choir as well.

Tuesday, June 30, 1942

This morning, dining room duty. Thereafter, Mrs. Ungeleider asked me would I like to perform some volunteer service duties. I said yes. Ilsinka and Karl paired up and I paired up with Lotte. One lady gave us biscuits. When we finished helping her, the other gave each one of us 5k. When we finished our tasks we were not too far from Aunt Stella's home so we dropped in. She coaxed us to stay a while as she was making special dumplings filled with strawberries and they are just great sprinkled with grated ginger mixed with sugar. Oh boy, just plain super! We returned home at 1:30 p.m. By the time we got to school it was 2:30 p.m., which meant that we got to skip at least our German class.

Wednesday, July 1, 1942

When I left school today, I met Lianka and she said to me, "You have a letter in my box from Ruzdka." So I rushed to get home. My aunt sent me two photographs, one of her, the other of our neighbors, the former mayor and his ladyfriend. It brought me such pleasure. Aunt Terka is really a fine person, she has concern for me. She fixed whatever needed attention and ironed everything so nicely. She also sent me all kinds of food. I will now have to sew on name tags and all the new-old things that just arrived. I think, however, that I will have a snack of something good first. In the meantime, Strap came in. It started to look as though it was going to rain. We quickly took everything in from the courtyard. Sure enough, soon after it came down. Ilsinka and I got busy setting up the tables again. We had potatoes, veal and beets for supper. Whoever wanted to, could also have some leftover cabbage from lunch. When I finished I went upstairs. Erma was there waiting to teach Strap, Cvok, Ilse and Lisa some English. I was just listening to them. Maybe some other time Erma will teach me also. Thereafter was bath time and time to go to sleep.

Thursday, July 2, 1942

Imagine, today we had free time for one whole hour. We were playing the harmonicas, me in particular. There is a Scottish song I like to play about the strahonic bagpiper. Then we had a lesson in Czek grammar and we had lots of fun. Our teacher, Mrs. Pick, asked Landsman to define the word philosopher. He said it meant being a neat hunter. Boy, did we laugh. Today school was cut by two hours and we went home earlier. We took the trolley instead of going on foot as we sometimes do, to get home quickly. I was going to get ready this and that when Ilsinka came in saying, "Don't bother, let Rose do whatever you have started. You and I have to go see Miss Weingarten's mother. She is in a transport, leaving soon and we are to bring back some things she cannot take with her. So I took off with her promptly. We had to go by the Bezrucove Gardens. I heard often how very beautiful it was inside. I had such a longing to go in to see, however, for us Jews, it was forbidden. We stopped off at my aunt's again.

Friday, July 3, 1942

Out of all my classmates, I like Ilsinka best. I always go with her to and from school. When she and I come home today, and I started to open the door, Helga was trying to do the same from the inside. Facing each other she said to me, "Milka, hasn't Honza come up to meet you? He went for you!" I got startled and hastily uttered, "Why, when, where? Oh no, have I received a summons? Is that why he went to meet me, to tell me that I have to go?" All these thoughts were flashing through my head. Fortunately that was not so. Soon Miss Weingarten entered and said to me, "Go eat something quickly, you and Honza have to go to the Federation to pick up some things." Was I ever relieved! I rushed to wash up, combed my hair and polished my shoes, wanting to look good and ran down to meet Honza. We took the streetcar and he would not let me pay, saying that he was given car fare for both of us by the director. He told me to put my money away. I let him pay but did not believe that money was given to him (it probably was so). Still on our return trip I hurried and paid for both of us. So that was that. What could he do? We had gotten a good meal while at the Federation. It was delicious. We were back home for a short while when I decided to go to buy some necessities for the eventual transport. Earlier that day I wrote a letter to Aunt Terka while still in school. We had a magician today in class to entertain us but he did nothing for me. I picked up a book and read instead and so those were the events of the day.

Saturday, July 4, 1942

I dreamt about Honza. Came the afternoon, I accompanied Ilsinka and Ervin Fleischer to the old folks home where Miss Weingarten's mom lived. We had to pick up more bags. We had to go across Jindrichove Namesti and around the Bezrucove Gardens once again. I liked so much whatever little I could see from the outside. Too bad that we are not allowed inside. For lunch was a casserole dish. Before that, Lianka and I took a bath and washed our hair. In the afternoon I took Ilse's place to be on dining room duty and help with this and that so that Ilse could leave earlier for a visit with her mom. When I finished cleaning up and prepared for later on, I left to visit my aunt. She gave me lots of different things. I ate their good knockwurst, potatoes an cabbage. Later on I had my second dinner in the orphanage. Then we had a sing-a-long. Otherwise nothing eventful.

Sunday, July 5, 1942

I didn't go anywhere today. Polda was in Ostrava today. He had to register. I didn't feel like going without him to Flora. It was terribly hot. I was lying in the courtyard and was reading. The sun was shining and the boys were playing volleyball. Others were wading through the kiddie pool. Otherwise nothing doing.

Monday, July 6, 1942

We are not learning anything in school these days. This is our last week. Some days we stay in only for 3 hours.

Tuesday, July 7, 1942

Today we took class photos. I kept looking straight at the photographer when suddenly the bulb blew up and sparks were flying everywhere. I have never seen anything like it. I got startled and closed my eyes. So if the photos should come out I will look as though I am asleep. That will look just great, I can't wait!

Wednesday, July 8, 1942

We are constantly getting ourselves and our things ready for **Terezin**. Mrs. Silberman is constantly sewing for us new things while we ourselves are fixing things we hope to take with us. Miss Beckova has some of our belongings prepacked in a state of readiness so that if we should God forbid, have to leave, there would not be too much last minute commotion. Yesterday she was getting me partially packed. I felt tired. My throat was hurting a bit and my head also. I figured that I better gargle with some phernagen. I didn't want my germs to spread and wanted to avoid being laid up. Marenka, Rutinka, Gerta and some of the boys are entering into a transport this Monday. I accompanied Gerta into the infirmary to have her bruised knee taken care of. I was getting tired and truly did not feel well. I took my temperature. It was almost 102, but I did not look flushed or feverish. In spite of it I had been in a good mood and had an appetite. I laid down in the sick room. Erna was there lying in the bed next to me.

All and all we are doing fairly well. Mrs. Hecht brought the two of us a compote made with gooseberries and cherries. It is really very good. Erna gave up her dish of farina to me. I sure enjoyed it. The other children are having pressed meat. I am not allowed. I still have a temperature of 102. Afterwards, Erna and I were comparing our likes and dislikes when it comes to food, both our stomachs agree one hundred percent on what we like to eat.

Thursday, July 9, 1942

Ilsinka brought home for me my report card. I have this year the worst report card ever. I have eight "B's" and a "C" in German.

Report Card

I. Eichnerova

Behavior	Excellent	(1)
German Language	Good	(3)
Religion	Praiseworthy	(2)
Czek Language	Praiseworthy	(2)
Geography	Praiseworthy	(2)
Nature Study	Praiseworthy	(2)
Handwriting	Excellent	(1)
Arithmetic	Praiseworthy	(2)
Geometry	Praiseworthy	(2)
Music	Excellent	(1)
Physical Education	Excellent	(1)
Sewing, Knitting, Embroidery	Praiseworthy	(2)
Drawing—Art	Excellent	(1)
Neatness	Excellent	(1)

Lianka finished the school year with very good marks. She got four 2's, otherwise all 1's. Cinda has two 3's. Among the boys Otta Jakubovic all 1's. Lacy the same as Strap.

Summer school vacation has arrived. It will not be a very happy time for me this year. Well, it cannot be helped.

Friday, July 10, 1942

We had an awful lot of fun yesterday. The older girls who have the larger bedroom make it a practice to share with one another whatever they get. Erna in particular. One girl in that group named Juta had a couple of boxes of shoe polish. While sitting on Finka's bed she opened them up. The polish was hardened and cracked, so small pieces fell out on the bed. This gave Juta an idea. The polish was brown so it was a perfect prank to put a small piece on Finka's pillow and as well as on the other pillows. As soon as Finka came upstairs, she went over to her bed and reaching out towards the pillow, grabbed the small brown piece saying, "And who do I have to thank for this?" She shoved a small piece into her mouth and found out fast that she had no chocolate treat, thus spit it out quickly. The poor thing rushed to brush her teeth and kept on rinsing her mouth vigorously trying to get rid of the shoe polish aftertaste.

Saturday, July 11, 1942

I am still running fever. Other than that, I feel good, thank God. Erna and I are very compatible sick mates. We kid around a great deal to help time to pass. Yesterday's dinner consisted of spinach, frankfurter potatoes but all I was allowed to eat was zwieback and something to drink. Mrs. Hecht always brings us some compote from the kitchen when Brauska is not there to look. As the week went by, the food got better. We had meat a couple of times with dill sauce, even fried cauliflower and a nice tomato.

Wednesday, July 15, 1942

Nothing new to report about me. Nonetheless, there is news. Cinda received her summons. She will be going to visit her father before she leaves. I will miss her and feel sad. Actually I am mad as hell. Pretty soon nobody will be here. Ella, Olga, Lia, Hana and also Margot are going back home. Not only for summer vacation but for good. Now Cinda, Marenka, Rutinka and Gerta have to leave for transport. Well I am mad, mad, mad! I wish that I could go back to Ruzdka and be with Aunt Terka. I miss her. Last year at this time I was there. Everything was fine. I used to pick wild strawberries, go into the woods to look for mushrooms and also bring back wood and pine cones. I used to go to bathe in the Becva River, I rode my bike and went with Vera to her aunt's farm in nearby Korabka. They had an orchard there as well. We climbed trees, raked hay and made haystacks. We jumped and frolicked around and slept in the attic. We built outdoor fires and baked potatoes. When I think about all that, I feel so much poorer now, especially since I no longer have my mom. At that time, even though we were forced to live apart, she was still alive. The other day I dreamed about Aunt Terka. The dream was so real that when I woke up I was so happy and lively that I started to jump around like a nut. I was in Ruzdka visiting her. It was so great. No one can comprehend my longing, no one, not even you, my Dear Diary. In spite of not liking it here nearly as well, I have to thank God and be grateful, for still being here. I just found out that Ruth Newbaur's mom has been notified that her time came to be deported. Ruth was not summoned, so she went voluntarily to request that she be allowed to leave but who knows if they are going to take her.

I kept busy writing letters this morning to Aunt Erna and to Zdenka. Then I did some sewing. Afterwards I will read parts of Verka's Diary. Jarka was trying to entertain herself by modeling dresses. The day before yesterday I had a visit from Aunt Ida, she brought me some dessert. She said that Leosek and Verushka were also laid up with some bug.

Prague, Thursday, July 16, 1942

Dear Milca,

I am writing to you on the day of my departure to Terezin.

Little one, I hope that you will always remain as kind, sincere, honest and good to the other children as you were when I first met you.

I will always remember you with gladness. We have not spent a great deal of time together but what we did have was good.

Honor the dear ones you still have, while you have them enjoy. When the day comes and you will have to face things alone, do not lose your head and your courage.

Think of me at that time and remember that I went resigned yet confident all by myself into the unknown.

When you read this I hope that you will think of me with happy thoughts and do so often thereafter.

Your

Cinda

Praha 16.VII.1942.

Moje milá Milčo!

Píši Ti to v den odjezdu do Teresíen-
stadtu...
Buď holčička vždy takova jak jsem
Tě poznala. Upřímná, prodomluv-
ná, čestná, hodná k ostatním dětem
atd.
Budu na Tebe vždy s radostí vzpo-
mínat. Prožili jsme spolu málo-
hezkých dní, ale přece!
Važ si Tvých milých, dokud
je máš. Až budeš sama, neztrácej
hlavu a buď statečná.
Vzpomeň si vždy na mně, která
šla odhodlaně a pevnou vůlí vpřed
sama a neví kam.

Až toto budeš číst, doufám, že si
často a ráda na mně vzpomeneš...
Tvá...
Cinda.

Letter from Cinda

Saturday, July 18, 1942

I am feeling okay. Betka comes over in the evenings and plays checkers with Erna. Eva got sick also so they put her in here with us. She sleeps a lot and when she is awake she plays harmonica on and off. I have been trying to read a little the works of Jiri Wolker and wanted also to get started on "Memories" by Carolina Svetla. I figured I would learn something, however it doesn't interest me too much. Well, I'll try one more time. Maybe if I begin to understand it I will start liking it as well.

Today at noon we had some kind of soup with meat and noodles and cauliflower, then French potatoes, which are made with salami and eggs. I was eating lunch when Miss Beckova handed me a letter from Uncle Gustav in which he wrote that Aunt Adele was summoned and already left with a transport. I truly felt bad.

I had a visitor yesterday. It was nurse Mina, who used to take care of mom when she was ill. Then I received a letter from Drazka. I was glad and had a laugh because she wrote that her boy cousin, Jara, arrived for a visit and Jira who is now vacationing in Ruzdka was real curious about him. However, he thought that she was a conceited little goose. Drazka wrote that Jira is very stuck on herself, that she shaved her eyebrows and painted her lips. I think that is so comical, why she is only 13 years old. A while back when she and I were friends, she was a great kid, then when I got to know Zdenu, she started to act false towards me and thought a lot of herself. That was for sure. By the way, we composed a great new song. It is not finished yet. Oh yes, it is aimed at Becka. It goes like this:

She entered the room at
dusk the scarecrow that she was

With chattering teeth she announced
that laziness she can not condone.

"From here I must get away
unless I can teach you to obey!"

She walked over to bed number one
and in her shrill voice said, "Get up,
You and everyone!" Those who will not
come downstairs soon, will have special
duties to perform at noon."

The lazy heads paid no heed to her at all
for sleeping longer was their only goal.

So when they finally descended down the stairs,
Becka dealt them a blow.

From then on they listened and how!

Sunday, July 20, 1942

Well at last yesterday morning I was busy packing some things, which I wanted to send home. In the afternoon I went shopping. Otherwise nothing took place.

Wednesday, July 23, 1942

Yesterday I went to my aunt. In the afternoon went to buy things accompanied by Erma, Fini and Ilse. We went to Zitna. Afterwards I hung around in the courtyard.

Polda received a summons. His bags are already packed and tomorrow he is going in. Also poor Lacy is leaving. She looks so very sad.

Sunday, July 26, 1942

I walked with Alenka to her friend's house all the way up Kaprova Street. We had to circle around and go towards the Vltava River. The sun was beating on us and I was dead tired when I returned to the orphanage. Everyone was already sitting down and eating lunch. We had noodle soup, veal, potatoes, dessert and I had about five glasses of water. Polda went to the Herzes (Uncle Max, Aunt Ida and Leosek) for lunch. I was to have gone there later on but I really did not feel like it because of the heat. Later on Eva and I went to the cemetery and then we stopped off at Hagibor when Eva said, "Let's buy some lemonade." Just then we heard someone calling out, "Eva!" We turned around and saw Joza who said to us, "Please don't buy the lemonade and especially not the almond sticks. I got sick from them and threw up. Better get some ice cream." Joza and Eva had jackets which covered up the Star of David, so they could ride the trolley but I couldn't. So I decided to walk and visit my aunt first and made up to meet with them at the "Old Jewish Cemetery." That settled, we went our separate ways. Aunt Ida, Stela, Helenka and little Vera were not around. So my uncle made a nice snack for me and then I left.

When I got to the top of the cemetery I was surprised to find Marianna there but Joza and Eva were not in sight. I kept thinking to myself that they ran off somewhere but a half hour later, they showed up. They went looking for ice cream on Zitna and on Irska Street and then onto Wencelas Square. They finally got ice cream, also a pickle and beer. Then they got back onto a streetcar and came here to meet me. From here, we walked home together. For supper we had fish in a jellied broth. We then went out into the courtyard and stayed there till 9:00 p.m.

Monday, July 27, 1942

Yesterday (that is, Sunday) we had much fun. It was a full moon. Margit said to us, "Kids, don't get scared if you should see me wandering around during the night. I am a moon walker and when the moon is full like it is tonight, you must not speak to me when you see me walking around in my sleep, otherwise I may get hurt." I got scared thinking to myself, that is just what we need. What next? Liana and Ruth jumped promptly into their beds and kept saying that they will scare the other girls after everyone goes to sleep. I listened for a while and looked towards the window at the sky. The moon shone ever so brightly. I started to feel the sandman coming and shortly fell asleep. I have no idea how long I slept, when I woke up my cover was gone. I had a pillow for a cover instead. Ruth was standing at my bedside saying, "Holy Ghost, Holy Ghost." Sleepy-eyed as I was, I looked at her a bit startled and then suddenly it clicked in my head what we earlier talked about and I laughed. I saw Margita with her nice blond hair in a yellow nightshirt and with her arms stretched out trying to walk. She stumbled, woke up and carried on with a foul mouth because she had a string wrapped around her feet. Liana and Ruth truly worried about her, tried to be helpful for fear that the bright glow of the moon should not pull her to the window and who knows, she may even try to fly out and get hurt. Our laughter and her scolding out loudly woke up Rose. She was beside herself, jumped up saying, "What the heck is going on," and looking at the sight of Margita she kept saying, "Oh my, oh my." By then the rest of us were rolling with laughter all over the floor. Lianka, Ilsinka and the rest. When we calmed down, we each went into our own beds to sleep. By then it was almost midnight.

Wednesday, July 29, 1942

Today I went to my aunt in Zabehlic where I stayed from early morning until 6:30 p.m. When I got there and rang the doorbell, no one answered. I was about to climb over the fence into the garden, when Aunt Ida showed up. She was in the laundry room and did not hear the first ring. She gave me a nice slice of bread with marmalade. I took with me a book to read and stayed in her garden. Fortunately, I brought with me a pair of shorts so that I was able to change, once it got too hot. Leosek had volunteer duty all day till 6:00 p.m. so I saw him only for a few minutes. Uncle Max came home for lunch at noontime so we ate together. Good soup, new potatoes and meat patties and palatchinky for dessert, almost the same as crepes.

After we got through washing the dishes and cleaning up, we got dressed and Aunt Ida and I went shopping. Mid-afternoon we had a snack, bread and butter with mustard and black beer. Then I went back into the garden and watered the vegetables. Then we both sat down and embroidered monograms on handkerchiefs.

Thursday, July 30, 1942

I forgot to note that Polda, Laci, Tabak, Altfater and Weinberger whom I hardly know, left with a transport. Polda cried as he was saying goodbye to Uncle Max but when he left here, he had a smile on his face. However poor Laci, I felt so very sorry for him. He looked so sad, trying to hold back his tears so hard, till his face turned all red until he no longer could control himself giving way to tears, slowly, drop by drop. It was just so very touching. Tabak, a small, frail black haired boy looked also very pitiful. Let's hope that dear God will look after all of them. Keep them in good health and make sure that someday soon they will all return and be happy again! (And be with us or with others they hold dear).

I went to Bernardof with Margita to visit Juta. She was operated and they took out her appendix. Then I went over to the Schoen family for a visit. Later on I was busy mending socks. I played in the evening till 9:00 p.m. in the yard. Then we had choir practice with Rudi. Honza, Otta and Jirka were singing. "When I grow up I will be a sailorman" Then six girls were singing a song made famous by the Allonovy Sisters, Trixi, Fini and Ruth sang "Dostavenicko" by Schuman, Eva, myself and Betka sang "Traumerei" by Schuman.

Friday, July 31, 1942

I felt truly weird and out of sorts but I didn't want to say anything. Marianna, I and five younger children went to the old cemetery. Marianna played wiffle ball. I sat down next to Aunt Stella and Veruska, who just happened to be there. Afterwards Aunt Stella went to buy a few things. When she returned she brought us a snack. I was sitting down wearing two coats and Verushka's small blanket was covering my knees. We went home toward the evening. Before we left I received an invitation for Sunday dinner to my aunt's house. On the way back Marianna got stomach cramps, so we left her tagging behind at a slower pace. Then suddenly Alenka started throwing up. I think it must have been from the bread. It was very awful.

Do you know who Alenka is? She has been with us six weeks already. Trixi was assigned to look after here but she is often away and Mrs. Ungeleider said to me that she noticed how well I looked after Rita before she left for **Terezin** so since I no longer had her to look after, she assigned Alenka to me. I must say that she is a little spoiled (in fact a whole lot) and sometimes complains to her father about all of us here.

Saturday, August 1, 1942

I spent the entire day, that is, morning and afternoon, in the workroom with Rose. I managed to wash my hair and take a bath in between. When we finished I sat in the garden and mended some socks. After supper, around 9:00 p.m., we had our choir practice. When we finished, I went with Irene, Betka and Trixi into the locker room. We were looking for a few things of ours. Suddenly we heard some rustling and an owl-like sound, *hoo hoo*, is spreading and getting closer and closer. The next thing we know, something or someone is standing a foot away from us. Trixi and I are huddling and squeaking. Then Trixi went jumping ahead and paw, bumped into someone else's head. Just then we heard a laughter which gave Lianka away. Then a little while later we spotted a little red light flickering here and there. I got scared and crawled into the locker. Still scared, I darted out a little later grabbing Lianka around her neck hanging on to her for dear life. She said to me, "You go ahead first. I'll follow." "Oh no, nothing doing," I said, so she went first, then I, Irene and Betka. As we walked through the door someone started to throw pillows and God knows what. Once again we saw the red light. This time we could see that it was a flashlight in the hands of Karel, Ota and Arnost. Lianka and Betka started to punch them and they kept hitting the girls back. I stood behind Strap and kept screaming. At last we got out of there and happily back into our bedroom. We washed up and took the covers off our beds. Becka came in to turn out the lights saying to us, "Children be still, your voice carries and every word of yours can be heard downstairs." We quieted down quickly and Helga started to tell us some romantic tales until we fell asleep.

Sunday, August 2, 1942

Today I went into Flora where Aunt Stella lives. I found a note that I was to come to Uncle Max in Zabehlic. Sure, go from Flora to Zabehlic. Easier said than done. I had no idea how to get there from Flora. I knew of one way but that was from the orphanage through Nusle and Michle but I surely did not want to go back there. I asked around and finally got some directions and one hour later on foot, I managed to get there. Lunch was so good. We had soup, hare a la paprikash, potatoes, cucumber salad and a superb tort. We spent the afternoon in the garden and Leosek, Verushka and I kept splashing in the tub outside. Afterwards I did some knitting. Then we had coffee and babka at snack time. Though a bit fearful, I took the trolley home at 6:30 p.m.

Monday, August 3, 1942

Right after breakfast we had to wash five doors by the toilets. It was a grind and it took us an entire morning to do it. I was pooped. At lunch today, I had a hard time getting the soup down. We also had new potatoes with dill sauce. After lunch we went to Bernardi and then to Hagibor. We have to go there every Monday, Wednesday and Friday.

Tuesday, August 4, 1942

I went to Aunt Jenny to Kelleyova Street where she works and visited Erna also. She was there to recuperate from her tonsillectomy. My aunt and I went to get her some ice cream and afterwards my aunt who works many hours in the hospital, wanted to go home. She had her street car travel permit whereas I have left mine home. So I tore off the star from my dress and hopped on the car too. It was fairly crowded, still I found a seat while my aunt had to stand. Well, Miss Milca was comfortable sitting down and both my aunt and I had to turn our heads quickly into the opposite direction, so that no one should notice the grin on our faces. It was hard not to do.

Wednesday, August 5, 1942

Today we were not to go to Hagibor. I don't remember what I did.

Thursday, August 6, 1942

First thing this morning I wanted to go to Zabehlice. So I went to Miss Beckova to let her know that I was going. She said to me, "Where is your star?" "I have one on my jacket downstairs which I will be wearing," I said. "Well then go and get it and come up to announce to me that you are leaving." So I did as she asked and when I came back up she looked at me and said, "You know, that is a light weight jacket. Today is cool. You need something warmer." "Okay, I will put on a coat if you want me to." She said, "No, a full length coat will not be necessary, just put on a heavier jacket." I asked, "Do I have to come back upstairs again?" "No, you don't have to. Be sure to get back home by 6:30 p.m., bye." So that's how our conversation ended. I made a dash for this downstairs locker room. I took my jacket out of the locker and shoved it into Rose's locker wanting to make certain that Becka would not by some change get to see it. Then I took a jacket without a star from Ruth. Having lost my street car riding permit (which I did not let on to Becka), I was destined to walking and I really did not want to walk so very far. I looked around carefully when leaving so that *you know who* should not get to see me, gave Lianka a quick hug and dashed out in a hurry. I got back sooner than I thought I would and went to take a nice nap. It was late in the afternoon and suddenly someone dumped water on me. It figured that Leos would do something like that (and so there he was, visiting in the orphanage and without a star).

Friday, August 7, 1942

In the morning dining room duties, then we went to Hagibor. We spent the entire day there. We were playing treasure hunt. Afterwards, Mr. Soudek was having a rehearsal for *"Midsummer Night's Dream."* We were given some soup with dumplings and the orphanage sent two huge baskets with sweet rolls.

Saturday, August 8, 1942

I took a bath and had to do the wash. I had other chores to do as well. Afterwards went to Aunt Jenny's place. I had a good snack and fell asleep until 6:00 p.m.

Sunday, August 9, 1942

I went to Zabehlic. It was great. Aunt Stella and Verushka were also there. We sat outdoors and I read the book *"My Friend Dana."* Then Aunt Stella said that she was going to cook kale tomorrow. I told her that I liked that a whole lot, so she invited me to come to her house.

Monday, August 10, 1942

I went to the old cemetery yesterday, then noontime while at Aunt Stella's waiting for food to be cooked, Verushka and I played with the rabbits in the yard. We had for lunch beef soup with dumplings and cauliflower. Then potatoes and kale. After that my aunt surprised me with yeast dumplings. Some were filled with plums, others with apricots. She served them with melted butter. Boy, oh boy, was that good! I just love both these dishes so much, these type of dumplings and kale. Thereafter my aunt went to buy some things and Verushka and I went back to the cemetery. It started to rain, so we went to the Tabors to keep dry. Aunt Stella came back with a raincoat for Verushka, brought us bread, keksy (English butter cookies) and cocoa. I did not feel like going home alone. Gita, Martha and

Pipca were nearby and I waited to go back with them at 6:30 p.m. Miss Beckova said to me, "Aren't you late coming back, my dear?" Gita quickly stuck up for me. I tried to wiggle out of my predicament by saying, "I thought that you said that I could return by dinner time." "Well, no harm done but you know very well when you were told to come back." I felt uncomfortable and my blood was rushing towards my head. My face must have been red like a beet—a dead giveaway that I lied. After we had eaten dinner and I have taken care of Alenka as usual, I went to sweep the floor. Then while the others were still sitting around in the dining room listening to a gramophone, I walked over to Miss Beckova to tell her that I lied to her earlier, that I knew very well when to get back but really didn't want to be walking by myself all that distance and in the rain. So that's why I have waited for Gita and the others to go with. She said with a smile, "It's okay. I knew it all along that you knew too."

Tuesday, August 11, 1942

Claudi and I went this morning to the Carl's Health Center for x-rays. Afterwards we stopped off at the laboratory on Kelleyova Street where Aunt Jenny worked. I excused myself to her for not coming over to her place in the afternoon as I was already invited to be in Flora at Aunt Stella's. We had potatoes with tomato sauce, green beans and dessert. In the afternoon I read a book and then was sunning myself in "our" park.

Wednesday, August 12, 1942

I swept the floors in both bedrooms. That was in the morning. I had no work to do in the afternoon. So I went and asked Miss Beckova to give me something to do. I waited a long time. Finally I left with Ruth for the game room. A few minutes later Becka walks in saying, "What are you two doing in here? Don't you have any chores to do? On with you into the study hall." Weird, when I asked her to give me some work to do, she doesn't. When I am having some recreation and fun she gets all excited because I am not at work on something. She finally told me that I should knit some socks. My dear Diary, I keep on writing but all this time my mind is elsewhere. I keep thinking of Aunt Terka. She is getting married to Mr. Zamrsky. I wish her the very best, form the bottom of my heart. I want her to be content and happy. I feel badly that I owe her so much and have no idea how I will ever be able to repay her. Will it be a year or two from now? One can never repay a good deed, her taking care of me so well and living in fear during all that danger. But I would like to be able to give her back some money at least.

I have been awaiting a letter daily. It has been three weeks already since I got one. I keep asking Miss Weingarten if she got some mail for me and I myself am on a lookout for the mailman.

Thursday, August 13, 1942

I went to Schunpeter to pick up Jule's and Ruth's photos. Then I cleaned the game room. I swept and mopped up three bedrooms. Then I went to the sick room to see Helga and she handed me a letter. She had it since yesterday. I don't know how it got there. She forgot to give it to me earlier. Dear Diary, I am very happy Aunt Terka left Ruzdka and moved back to Vsetin. She said that she and her new husband got a nice apartment there. She said that someday I will come back and have a new home with them. Well, it will not be so nice since the home will not include my mom, but I know that she will try to make it up to me. I like her very much. I went to play in the afternoon in the courtyard. Then went to Aunt Jenny's where I ate so much, I thought I would burst.

Sunday, August 16, 1943

I went with Ilse yesterday to buy a pair of tennis shoes. She was wearing the star, I was not. We kept on laughing. Afterwards of course I went into the candy store and ice cream store as well. Then we went to Aunt Jenny. Somewhere I lost 4k and food stamps I had for rolls.

Today I went to Zabehlic to Aunt Ida's. We had a roasted rabbit, tomato salad and pishinger tort. In the afternoon we had cocoa and a piece of bundt cake. Afterwards Leosek and I went bike riding.

Thursday, August 20, 1942

I straightened out Alenka's closet before breakfast. Afterwards I studied. Liana, Ilse, Lisa and I are taking English lessons from Erna. When "Cvok" (Cinda) was still here, she too studied English. Ruth said that she also wants to learn. Then I rode to Zabehlic. Lucky one, I now have a riding permit that is good for 1½ months. I gave my aunt a hand in the kitchen. We had tomato soup today and cheese dumplings afterwards. When we got through washing the dishes we went to Botice where we managed to swim a little.

Saturday, August 22, 1942

Today is my first day of kitchen duty. This is how it came about. I spoke with Miss Weingarten the day before yesterday while she was showing me how to knit socks. I asked her to give me some chores to do and of course she had none for me. "How about giving me some of Liana's duties to do?" She said to me that I couldn't do them, that they would be too difficult for me to handle. So I said that I would like to assist in the kitchen. "Really, is that what you would like to do?" I said, "Ano" and that finished the conversation. I kept thinking about knowing that Ilse Freund was fed up already with her kitchen duty and wanted out. Still she did not have the guts to say so. Erna kept encouraging her. At last Ilse said openly that she had enough and did not mind at all letting someone else take over. Just then Miss Weingarten told me that Malva took ill and that I could handle her chores downstairs. I was glad.

Today we had schunken flackeln (diced ham with eggs and noodles) for lunch and potato salad for dinner. So I went to help dicing and mixing potatoes with mayonnaise, chopping pickles, carrots, wurst (deli meat) and tossing everything lightly and delicately together. I finished around 2:30 p.m., then ran off quickly to visit Aunt Jenny. She gave me bread, sugar and a sour pickle, also buttermilk which I enjoyed.

Sunday, August 23, 1942

Our bunch gets up usually earlier than the others. There were hardly any chores to do. We had soup with dumplings, beef and potatoes, also cheese tarts. Thereafter I had some ironing to do. Later went to my aunt again. I was told to be back at 6:30 p.m. but go back at 6:45 p.m. Miss Ungeleider said to me, "Next time you will have to be back at 5:30 p.m. Miss Weingarten has told me to keep an eye on you and to see when you get back. It seems that you were late on several occasions. What happened last time?" I kept silent. It was true. What could I have said? But nonetheless it got me mad as hell that I was reprimanded by her.

Monday, August 24, 1942

Today I tried to do some baking. I made some indents in the dough so that I had room to fill them with some jam or jelly. Then I polished off five of them. I messed up a lot of dishes and pans. Had a big cleanup to do. Well at least we have here in the kitchen plenty to do. Honza and I get into frequent fights. Yesterday he gave Erna an egg to hide. Later on he went looking for it but couldn't find it. When he came back I was holding the door shut, not allowing him to come in. He pushed and I couldn't hold out, so I let go and ran like a scared rabbit away from there. Just then Becka appeared out of nowhere. I didn't even say hello to her. I kept running with Honza right behind me. I made it only up to the dining hall. He grabbed me and I started to yell. Becka kept looking in bewilderment, not used to seeing me horsing around with Honza. We were fooling around and he tried to push me down to the floor and then sat on me. I did not like that at all and yelled even louder till I startled Ruth and Zdenka in the dining room.

I said to Honza, "You better let one go and right now or I will slap your face, yes I will!" He didn't believe me. No, I didn't slap him. I pinched him instead, as often as I could. Then he tried to hold my hands in back of me saying, "Tell me that you are sorry that you have pinched me, then I will let you go." Well, I didn't say sorry to him but pleaded with him saying that I will be real nice to him if he lets go of my hands. He dragged me further away into the dining room and there in a corner was a box. I screamed, "Honza, the egg, that's where Erna hid your egg. Go and see." He said, "No, you go and bring it to me." "Okay, okay, so let go of me already," and he did. I went to rescue the egg and brought it back to Honza. It was hollow inside and water was dripping from it all the way. I kept laughing harder and harder and he got mad again and started to rough-house all over again but not for long. "What did you do to the egg?" he said. I replied, "Looks like someone sucked out the yoke from it." "Not me, not me." The poor egg white went drip, drip. There was not much left of it.

Thursday, August 26, 1942

Yesterday I slept till 9:30 a.m. in the kitchen. Everyone went upstairs where Mr. Soudka was putting on the play *"Midsummer Night's Dream"* while I kept slaving away. After lunch today I kept on washing dishes. Then I had to go and fix the elastic in my shorts. Thereafter I went into the tub for a good scrubbing. I will go into the yard for a short while. I must hurry. Oli still needed help in the kitchen and got two boys to help her. I asked her to excuse me for a short while, as I really needed some air. I stopped in the yard for only 20 minutes sunbathing before going indoors again to help to prepare supper. One can tell these days that I am working in the kitchen. I have many finger cuts to prove it. Boy, I sure eat better here. You have to be smart and figure out angles in order to get more food. When no one is around I cut myself an extra slice of bread and I hide it in a neat place for later on. For lunch we had today cream spinach with a sunny up egg and potatoes. I got very hungry later, snooped around the kitchen and pigged out on leftovers.

Then Honza and I started to scrap around because I have hid his mop and pail. So Rudi came over to help Honza dump water on me to get even.

Dear, Dear Diary, for several nights now when I get into the bed I want to bawl my head off. I keep telling myself, "No, you mustn't, you are not a weakling." I don't get together with Lianka too much. In the mornings we are both very busy. In the afternoon she spends time with Ruth or is being entertained by Joza. She is really a neat girl and good to me. Some evenings I hop into her bed next to her and I feel good. We talk. I tell her what I am thinking and ask her for advice with things I don't know how to handle. She is like an older sister to me. When I tell her this and that, she explains the meaning to me. I am sorry to say that I am not her confidant, she is a little older and doesn't need me the way I need her. To me she is a sister and a good friend. From the way I write to you Diary, it seems to me that I miss some stroking, some tender, loving care and lots of hugs. I simply get overwhelmed with feelings I can not properly express. I think Lianka cannot express her feelings either. Well enough of that today. My Dear Diary, just want you to know that I did not even go into the yard today. I wanted to be with you and write all this to you. It is almost 10:00 p.m. I have to go to sleep now, so good night!

August 27, 1942

Today we got up earlier. Betka and I had to make pancakes for everybody. Then we had to wash the dishes after we got washed up, we rode to Hagibor. They were putting on a play. It came off very well and Mr. Soudek received a bouquet of flowers and promptly went to the cemetery to place it on his father's grave. Summons came this morning for Irene and Hana (her mother got one too) but none of us said anything to Irene since she was in the play, except for little Hans from the Kinder home, he came over to her saying, "Irenko, are you going to leave us for **Terezin?**" She flipped out instantly. Shortly thereafter Mr. Cenkr came over saying cheerfully, "See you in the deportation center, Irene!" The poor thing didn't know what to make of it. (He got a summons also). When the play was over as well as some celebration, she was informed that her time has come to leave with a transport. She broke down crying.

Tuesday, September 1, 1942

Today I was off, no dining room duty. The place needed a thorough scrubbing and general cleanup. Yep. I begged off. Honza came over to tell us that he too had to join in the transport. He kept saying that it really was so, on his honor, but he crossed his hands and looked sheepish.

Thursday, September 3, 1942

Yesterday morning and today I took off the entire day except for peeling potatoes in the kitchen. I went to Flora, where Aunt Stella lived for a visit. All of them are in the transport. I went to help and made a trip to Zabehlic to get a carton. Then I sat down and did some knitting.

Friday, September 4, 1942

I stayed in the kitchen until 3:00 p.m. Then I washed two of my blouses, shorts, a shirt and two pairs of pants. Afterwards I washed my hair and took a bath. As luck had it, we had warm water for a change. Afterwards I had some bread and drank some buttermilk. By then it was 5:30 p.m., at which time I was heading for Olsany. I went via Straslice to the cemetery. I bought my momma peonies and the woman I bought them from added a few carnations. Thereafter I went to the Schlesners, so that we could say goodbye. Aunt Stella gave me some fruit to take back, which I shared in the evening with Strap.

Saturday, September 5, 1942

Today we were saying goodbyes to Ota Jacubovic, Petr Frank, Dolly, Mariana, Margit and her mother, Gita, Martha and their mother, our best choir singer Trixi (829) and some boys who were newcomers to our home. Also the personnel was leaving at this time. Oly (13f567), both Gretas, Lotte, not to forget Karel Eisner who left earlier.

We had for lunch French style potatoes and tomato salad. Afterwards I went to visit Aunt Jenny. She was not at home. So I went to Aunt Helenka where I had coffee with two apricot danish, also a slice of tort which I took back with me. She asked me to return tomorrow but I don't know how to manage that since I made a definite date with Aunt Jenny.

Dear Diary, Aunt Stella, Martha and Helenka are not my real aunts, only Jenny and Ida. Stella is Aunt Ida's sister (Ida is married to my uncle). The others are the wives of Ida's brothers. I just call them all aunts, it gives me a sense of family.

Thursday, September 9, 1942

Today I got up early because I had to be at Aunt Jenny's at 8:00 a.m. Today was her daughter's funeral. After the trip to the cemetery I hung around for a while, then came back home. Some man by the name of Fabian was getting married, so our group went to sing for the wedding. They gave us 4 torts, to divide among ourselves. In the afternoon I had kitchen duty once again.

Sunday, September 12, 1942

I spent the entire morning in the kitchen again. In the afternoon Lianka and I were horsing around. We took the trolley to **Letna** where the girls' orphanage used to be before merging with the boys' orphanage on **Vinohrady**. We just looked around and then went on to the **Hradcin castle**, to the ground area called the **Elk's Ditch**. There are trees and grass and huge rocks there and the water runs through the opening in the rocks. There are also two bears roaming around there. Thereafter we went to the tower where we had to climb some 240 stairs. At the very top of the tower is a huge bell. From that point we feasted our eyes on the magnificent panoramic view of Prague we call the Mother City. Then we walked over to the Saint Vitus Cathedral. Unfortunately we didn't get to see the rest of the complex. We spent a total of four wonderful hours there.

No more kitchen duty for me. School has already begun a while back but we are no longer allowed to attend. So we find some comfort in being able to listen to some lectures here. At least we have something. I am not able to go downstairs any more. That section is closed off now. I keep myself busy with knitting, reviewing old assignments and studying some English, which I truly enjoy. Last night I felt very sick. I came down with diarrhea and was throwing up. So I had to go to stay in the sick room and I was put on a diet.

Monday, September 1942

Today is *Yom Kippur*. I am fasting a half day only. Aunt Jenny came to visit me in the infirmary.

Wednesday, September 22, 1942

I have a severe case of sore throat and a 103 degree fever. It sure hurts—my tonsils are infected. In three weeks, should I still be here, they will be taken out. Betka is laid up also. She is in the bed next to me. When it starts getting dark, we turn on our light. Our beds are by the window. Honza is on the second floor and talks to us from the window in the toilet. We look up, he looks down, or else Betka and I play a guessing game about cities and countries they are in. We also read. Tomorrow I will be able to get up for a while and stay up.

I came to the end of my 2nd Diary. Perhaps I will write someday again. I just received a package from home with some goodies from the wedding.

And now I end with a parody of a Czek song patterned after "*Andulko, me dite*," which goes like this.

> *Ilsinko, my dear girl*
> *I like you very, very much.*
> *Ilsinko, my dear girl, you are so neat.*
>
> *Dear Honza, I must say*
> *that people are not glad for me,*
> *that I care, always did*
> *wanting to go steady with you!*

On The Subject Of God And Survival

It was that of a believer, during my horrendous ordeal, for no matter what has befallen me in life, I needed to know that I was not alone, even though it seemed that way at times. That there was someone to whom I could address my thoughts to. Someone I could plead with and even come to question. This helped, even if only temporarily, to distract me from my present pain and anguish, as it brought me a few minutes of relief, if not a solution. Sometimes when anger and hopelessness gave way to my thoughts I kept on talking to Him. Did He answer or fix things? No! Yet in a way an answer did come to me which was in the form of the realization that for the present I had to rely on my own resourcefulness, thus I thanked Him for making me aware of that.

There was a time however, when I did stop believing in the kind and ever loving God. Nothing that was happening around me made any sense anymore, nor did it ever before but I fought it with the memories of home life. Such as the warmth of the Sabbath and other holidays and of the various dishes my mom had made. I did some tasting and experienced imaginary cooking through involvement with others who did likewise which helped a great deal. Knowing of the ongoing war and the involvement of the Americans, I turned my prayers to them for I was convinced that the Americans and only the Americans were going to free us from our slavery and misery. I had a rude awakening one more time as I had fallen into the Russian sector, after being on the German death march from which I managed to escape. Thus freeing myself with God watching over me.

Ústí 19.III.-46

Meine liebsten!

Heute sende ich Euch mitt grosser Freude einen Brief, über welchen Ihr Euch sicher auch freuen würdet. Ich war 1 Woche in Prag und bin gestern zurück gekommen. Ich bin schon entlich registriert unter Nummer 152. Amerik. konsulat sendet angeblich alle die Dokumenten nach Waszhington. Bitte fraget nach. Jetzt habe ich alle Dokumenten bei sammen, ich warte also nur auf die Schieffskarte, die ich von Euch aus U.S.A. bekommen muss. Ich habe gehört, dass die erste auschaffüng soll in Jüni abreisen ü. zwar die Nümmer bis 300 (da zwischen gehöre ich,) die andern erst in Herbst.

Liebste Tante u. Onkel
ich bin sehr neugierig, wie wir uns
erkennen. Ich trage
Eure l. schöne Bilder,
bei mir. Aber trozdem,
soll ich mir nicht eine Tulpe, oder
irgendwelche Blume in die Hand
nehmen? Ich möchte aber lachen,
wenn noch irgedeins Mädchen den
selben Einfall hätte und Ihr dann
zu Ihr geht anstadt zu mir. (In
wirklichkeit fürchtige ich mich
nicht, ich mache nur einen Spaas)

Ich warte immer sehr ungedul-
tig auf Euren Brief, der mir
immer so viel Freude bringt.
Ich bin unnentbaar glücklich
dass der l. Gott zu mir so brav
war und das ich Euch wieder
nach so lange Zeit schreiben

March 19, 1946

My dear ones!

Today I am sending you with great joy a letter which will make you happy as well. I spent one week in Prague and returned yesterday. Finally, I was registered and was given the number 152. At that time, the American Consulate forwarded all my papers to Washington. Please follow up at your end. Since I have now all the documents together, the only thing that is needed is for you to send me the ship ticket which must come from the U.S.A. I have learned that the first group here will be leaving in June. The call will be issued for numbers up to 300. The others will be leaving later on in the fall, I was told.

I am curious how we are going to recognize each other. I carry your precious photos with me daily but even so, shouldn't I have a tulip or some other flower in my hand? I am laughing to myself thinking, wouldn't it be funny if some other girl had the same thought that I had and you went over to her instead of me? (Just so that you know, I'm truly not afraid, just kidding around).

I am always anxiously awaiting your letters and thank God for having been given the opportunity to be in touch with you once again after such a long time.

(Letter was written by Ilse to her aunt and uncle in the USA. The letter was written in German as Ilse's aunt and uncle didn't speak Czech.)

111

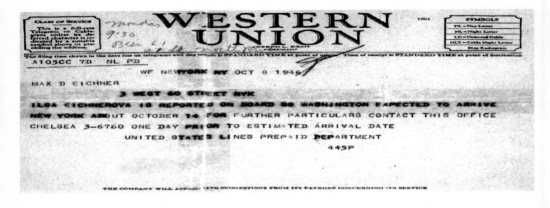

At long last, I arrived in the United States, bringing shadows of the past with me.

I enjoyed my family and newly found freedom for which I was most grateful and later on went on to making a family of my own. Years went by and in the Spring of 1995 I journeyed back to my homeland to attend the **50th Anniversary of the liberation of Terezin.**

Fiftieth Anniversary Gathering
Closing Statement

It was in May of 1995, when I boarded the plane leaving Zurich, Switzerland, where I spent a few hours sightseeing. I got on a plane once more with destination being Prague. I did so with much apprehension and yet compelled to do so. It was simply unthinkable not to go, for the occasion was the **fiftieth anniversary gathering of the Theresienstadt survivors, commemorating the liberation and the ending of WWII.**

I was met at the airport by friends I have not seen nor heard from in fifty years. They were the former children and my roommates from the **Kinder Heim L410, room 24—Terezin.** Their names were **Helga Weissova/Hoskova,** the child artist whose sketch and diary excerpts can be found in *I Never Saw Another Butterfly* and **Marta Laskova/Kottova.** Another dear friend, **Ruth Justitzova/Haasova** residing with her husband in Frankfurt, Germany, had to cancel on short notice.

Terezin child artist Helga Weissova/Hoskova sitting down and looking up at Miluska (Ilse) who is standing up looking at photo of herself that Helga brought having kept it for 50 years.

Marta Laskova/Kottova

That night in Prague I slept poorly. The next morning Marta and I got up early (I stayed in her apartment) and took a taxi to a bus terminal in another sector of Prague known as Holesovice. There we were greeted by other survivors not known to me except for five. We got on the charted buses with destination, **Terezin**. How happy I was when I spotted my cousin Polda (known today as Leo Lowy) and his wife Evelyn from Hackensack, New Jersey. Seeing them brought a measure of comfort, as we got into our seats and I reflected on the "cattle cars" with guards all around us, some half a century ago.

We met the other former inmates upon our arrival through the picturesque Czech countryside, with fields of sprawling yellow flowers everywhere. Among those attending were eighty out of the one hundred surviving children, having come from as far as Australia. We gazed intensely into each others faces trying to recognize in these aging people (many of whom were grandmothers by now), the twelve, thirteen and fourteen year old children we once were. There was some recognition but what there was most of, was an element of disbelief that all this was taking place, yes it was real!

On that day the sun was shining every so brightly and as the band started to play the Czech national anthem **'Kde Domov Muj, Kde Domov Muj"** translated "Where Is My Home, Where Is My Home."

Band playing at ceremony.

The tears streamed down my face as I joined in singing and remembered the anthem sang by me years ago, when I was a happy, carefree school child, living in the country I loved so much. I looked ahead and saw so many small grave markers and there to the right stood a *Menorah*. Further down to the left of me was the *Star of David*, erected on a pole, very high at that. Not too far from me was another pole, this one bearing the cross and was but a short distance from the notorious **Little Fortress**, known for horrors inflicted upon Jews and Christians alike.

I knew then why I had to come. To show solidarity and give thanks for my life.

I will never go back again, nor will I ever forget!

Shalom,

Miluska (this is the name I gave myself while in the orphanage and it has remained with me throughout the various camps. I was also called at times Milka or Milca).

EPILOGUE

Sixty years have passed since the Holocaust atrocities and the ending of WWII. The survivors are getting old; in fact many of them have died. Their spirit goes on living in our hearts. We built memorials and educate the children of the future generations by going to schools or having them come to the museums of Jewish heritage. We tell our stories and paint images with our words for those who care to know more about our plight and historic accuracy.

We speak of faith and courage but also in some cases, of incredible luck and emphasize tolerance. I personally focus on the fact that there is no difference between the color of blood among races or various religious groups and state how the physical cruelties and mental anguish go together. If not checking and taking preventative measures in proper time, we contribute towards hurt, disappointments, anger and hate. Once we allow the last one to occur, we are in deep trouble, for hate destroys! So although we can not always love or even like everybody, we have no right to hurt people or animals for that matter either. The golden rule being, "Do not do unto others, what you would not like them to do unto you!"

So simple, why can it not work?

*Photo of Ilse taken in June 2004 in the same place as the
picture on the cover of the book, only 64 years later.
In Ruzdka
today known as Bystricka*

Speaking Engagements

*Ilse holding the diary in her hand upon having
completed her presentation to the school children at Kennesaw.
(next to her sits the classroom teacher)*

Ilse's speaking engagements include the Rotary Club International in Atlanta, the William Breman Jewish Heritage Museum, Emory University, Kennesaw High School Magma Group, Los Angeles Middle School, Patrick Henry Middle School in Stockbridge, Georgia and various drama study institutions.

Ilse's first speaking presentation was the most bewildering of all. While on her first visit to her homeland in 1990, she met up in the Jewish section of Prague with the Rev. John Ekman from Sarasota Springs, N.Y. who with his wife and teachers, brought along the youth from the Presbyterian Church.

In the fall of 2004 a short TV film was featured nationwide in the Czech Republic of her reminiscences during her childhood years under the Nazi regime, filmed with her in her hometown. A radio show is planned next.

Glossary

Aryan (Other than Jewish) term used by the Nazis during WWII.

Auschwitz A notorious concentration camp in Poland— "Oswetim"

Bima Jewish for pulpit.

Bohemia Historic province of Czechoslovakia.

Brocha Name for a Jewish blessing.

Brno Also known as Brünn, capitol city of Moravia, which together with Bohemia comprised Czechoslovakia.

Challa Braided loaf of bread used by Jews on Sabbath and holidays other than Passover.

Gestapo German secret police during the Nazi era.

Hagibor A Jewish recreation center.

Heimish Warm, friendly.

Jitzkor Jewish prayer for the deceased.

Jom Tov Greeting on Jewish holiday.

Megillah   A long tale, story.

Mogen David   The six pointed Star of David, symbol of the Jews.

Moravia   Province of Czechoslovakia, now Czech Republic.

Passover   Holiday celebrating the Jewish passage of freedom from the Egyptian slavery.

Ravensbrück   First women's concentration camp in Mecklenburg, Germany (at first for political prisoners).

Sabbath   The Jewish day of rest—starts Friday at sundown and ends Saturday at sundown.

Seder   Passover dinner with rituals, songs and blessings during which the children ask questions about the symbolism pertinent to that night.

Spielberg   A notorious medieval castle complex in Brno—Moravia used as a cruel prison in past history. Now a museum housing paintings.

Terezin   Also known as Theresienstadt—ghetto for Jews in the former Czechoslovakia, a transit camp to labor and extermination camps in Poland, mainly Auschwitz/ Birkenau.

Torah   The Jewish scroll which includes the five books of Moses.

CPSIA information can be obtained at www.ICGtesting.com
Printed in the USA
LVOW061734250712

291532LV00007B/153/A